Fly Fishing

FOR SUMMER STEELHEAD

JOHN SHEWEY AND FORREST MAXWELL

Frank Amato
PORTLAND

MW00862319

FRANK AMATO

©1996 by John Shewey and Forrest Maxwell

All rights reserved. No part of this book may be reproduced without the express written consent of the publisher, except in the case of brief excerpts in critical reviews and articles.

All inquiries should be addressed to:
Frank Amato Publications, Inc., P.O. Box 82112, Portland, Oregon 97282
(503) 653-8108
Photos and illustrations by John Shewey unless noted otherwise.
Book and Cover Design by Kathy Johnson
Printed in Canada
1 3 5 7 9 10 8 6 4 2
ISBN: 1-57188-028-3

Contents

FRANK AMATO

Introduction

This book arrived by way of several years of frustration on our part: For years, while working at the fly shops, we listened to the woes of beginning fly anglers or experienced trout anglers expressing dismay at the thought of learning to catch steelhead on a fly. We did our best to quiet their fears, which were typically born out of a kind of intimidation. This intimidation resulted—and results—from a perusal of the voluminous steelheading literature on the market today.

While much of this literature offers excellent information, very little is directed specifically at the entry-level steelheader. Thus the fly fisher who thinks about making the leap to steelhead angling is met head-on by a lot of sometimes-tedious, sometimes-conflicting and frequently complicated information. Yet fly fishing for summer steelhead is a decidedly simple form of fly fishing: We need not match hatches, study entomology, perfect drag-free drifts, land fish on fine tippets or burden ourselves with other complexities inherent to fly fishing for trout.

So if fly fishing for summer steelhead is comparatively simple, why should the beginner feel intimidated? After years of fishing and years of observation we have come to believe that three primary factors account for the "unapproachability" of steelhead fishing: First, steelhead are fish of legend here in the Northwest—so much so that to land steelhead on a fly long ago became a kind of high-water mark for fly anglers. Secondly, the legendary status of this wonderful gamefish, coupled with the high esteem in which successful steelhead anglers are held by the angling community, leads quite naturally to the over-involvement of ego. When ego gets in the way of instruction and in the way of the passing on of knowledge, the recipient of such communication sometimes ends up thinking along these lines: "If it takes a great angler like him to take steelhead on a fly, how can I hope to achieve any success?"

We have heard this line, in various form, uttered over and over by fly anglers who, for that very reason, hesitate to immerse themselves in the wonderful world of steelheading.

This leads to the third factor that prevents potential recruits from diving head-long into steelhead fly fishing. Over the years we have heard many folks say that the idea of maybe hooking one steelhead in a day or in a week simply does not justify the efforts when during the same time period one might hook dozens of trout. For every person who has openly said as much to us, we would guess another 10 harbor these same feelings. Certainly such anglers have every right to make that choice. However, these feelings seem to be a natural part of the transition for many if not most people who take up steelhead angling.

The angler who makes that choice after having hooked and landed several steelhead is doing so with eyes open. We submit, however, that the angler who prefers trout fishing without first giving steelhead angling a fair shake misses out on some of the best that our sport has to offer.

Since you have taken the step of reading this far, we assume you want to catch steelhead on a fly. As you read on, you will no doubt come to see just how simple this game really is despite a reputation to the contrary. We suggest that you not make steelhead angling a numbers game. We believe whole-heartedly that the opportunity to fish some of the world's most beautiful rivers and the privilege to occasionally hook a steelhead on a beautiful fly far outweigh the number of fish we catch. Quite frankly, we don't count fish. We don't care about that. We believe it is the fish counters amongst fly fishing's ranks who have been largely responsible for creating an aura of unapproachability around the fine sport of steelhead fly fishing. For such people the number of fish brought to the beach supersedes the fishing itself. They use whatever technique yields the most results for the least effort.

We hope this book will give you two things: The information you need to catch steelhead and the desire to do so in a "gentlemanly" manner. The ends do not justify the means so far as we are concerned, so we will not pursue steelhead with weighted nymphs under indicators, with lead-head leeches, articulated leeches or any of the other of the nouveau methods that have invaded this fine sport for the sole purpose of putting fish on the beach with as little investment of time and effort as possible.

In fact, the angler who disdains the traditional methods of steelhead fly fishing necessarily robs him or herself of the sport's most endearing aspects—intimate familiarity with the stream arrived at through days and years of wading miles and miles of classic steelhead water and covering said water with cast after cast, each one delivered downstream of the previous one. By fishing in the traditional manner as we describe it in this book, you cannot help but better your understanding of the nature of a river and you cannot help but become a better caster, better wader and we believe a better person.

Steelhead fly fishing offers you something of a spiritual revival: After a long incarceration in the world of work, traffic, taxes and other such depressants, you find yourself on an elegant summer steelhead stream, its pristine waters curling gracefully and wild around your legs as you enter at the top of a long pool. The first few casts shake off the rust from your hiatus from fishing and by the tenth or twelfth cast, you start to notice things: The gentle fog clinging to the tops of the towering fir trees that act like sentinels

Ken Hanley with a Deschutes River summer steelhead.

for the river; the water ouzels doing their inquisitive little dance on the moss-cloaked river rocks. A few more casts and you remember how that wonderful "swish . . . swish" of your airborne fly line seems a part of the river, perfectly in tune with the tumbling riffle above and the swirling currents surrounding your waders. After each cast, you study the fly line as it marks the path of your fly swinging across the currents. Some time later you have reached the tailout of this pool, where the water flows glassy and smooth before pouring gently into the riffle below.

No steelhead come to the fly in this pool and you don't really care. The river itself and your sense of belonging are enough. Perhaps the next pool or the one after that will yield a fish. The world of ringing phones, televisions and other modern distractions is forgotten for now and you relish the knowledge that somewhere in this river, maybe today, maybe tomorrow or the next day, a steelhead will humor you by grabbing your fly, an act which will only heighten what has already been a day too perfect for words.

Fly fishing at its finest. Such is steelhead fly angling for us and we hope this book will help you enjoy steelhead fly fishing as much as we do.

John Shewey and Forrest Maxwell *January, 1995*

Some steelhead in southern Chile are extremely heavy for their length. This fish was photographed quickly and released for scientific purposes.

FRANK AMATO

Chapter 1

The Confidence Factor

John Shewey with a Deschutes River steelhead. Rick Wren photo.

Confidence may well be the most significant attribute of the successful steelhead angler. Confidence transcends technique and strategy. More than that, confidence elevates your angling skills because it instills in you a belief that there exists no doubt about the fact that you will catch a steelhead. Unburdened by doubt, you come to decide that casting, wading and reading water are skills at which you will tirelessly try to better yourself.

Any doubts about hooking steelhead are pushed far out of your mind. As you deliver each cast there exists not a doubt in your mind that a steelhead will grab the fly on that presentation. When this fails to happen you are nothing short of flabbergasted; absolutely aghast that a fish did not pounce on the fly. So dumbfounded are you that your confidence doubles on the next cast. If again a fish fails to grab the fly, you find yourself entirely astounded. Never does your confidence wane—no matter how many casts, how many hours or how many days pass without a hookup. Conversely, your confidence builds in proportion to your astonishment. Your reasoning is simple; fundamental. How can there exist any doubt that the next cast will take a fish since the last 50 have failed to do so?

In short there is no doubt. Doubt never enters the confident steelheader's mind. In this way, confidence makes us better anglers. We concentrate fully on our efforts: When our fly hangs in the currents directly downstream at the end of the swing we stand there in the river entirely befuddled that a steelhead did not give chase. Then we can't wait to make the next presentation because we are more certain than ever that the forthcoming cast will take a fish.

So enter into your steelheading days with utter confidence. Concentrate on learning and perfecting the techniques described in this book; practice your casting, wading and water-reading skills; fish as often as you can. Through all of this, believe in every cast. You will catch steelhead on a fly.

Chapter 2

Assembling Your Tackle

A few years ago we were sitting around the fly shop at noon on a summer day, taking a break from our duties of handling phone orders, packaging materials, tying flies and talking fly fishing. A fellow wandered in looking for a few flies for his upcoming steelhead trip to Oregon's Deschutes River. Nothing seemed out of the ordinary about the situation except that this angler wanted his flies tied on a number eight hook.

Granted, No. 8's will take fish on the Deschutes, but we've always had better success beaching those tough Deschutes steelhead with slightly larger hooks. Further along in the conversation, we learned why this fellow wanted No. 8's: He intended to fish the river with a three-weight rod. Neither of us jumped on our soap box at this revelation, but we tried fairly diligently to persuade our customer that a three-weight is less than ideal for steelhead fishing.

Now that might seem rather obvious to most folks. After all, tactically speaking, a light trout rod doesn't give you much leverage against an eight- or ten-pound steelhead in a big, swift river. But the tactical considerations were not our main concern. More importantly, at least to our way of thinking then and now, is the concern for the well-being of the steelhead itself. A light trout rod will indeed handle a steelhead, but only if the angler on the business end has a fair amount of patience. In other words, our fellow bent on fishing the three-weight would have to battle a steelhead for far too long in order to beach the fish.

Such a drawn-out battle cannot help but tire the fish unnecessarily and thus casts considerable doubt over whether that fish, even after released, will live to see another day. That is our major objection to the use of light tackle on steelhead, the only exceptions being the small "half-pounder" sized fish of the Rogue River and a few other waters.

Beyond such philosophical reasons, we would never choose trout-sized rods anyway. They simply make the entire process of steelheading more difficult. A seven-, eight- or nine-weight rod will cast farther than a trout rod, will perform better in the wind, and will handle steelhead far more successfully.

We are not suggesting that the beginning steelhead angler must immediately run out and drop $400 on a new steelhead rod. If you already own a six-weight trout rod, by all means begin with that. If and when you can justify the cost of a new rod, then do indeed run out and cast a few eight- and nine-weights until you find one that feels right. We generally opt for nine-weight rods. They tame the wind, they cast a long line and they handle steelhead efficiently.

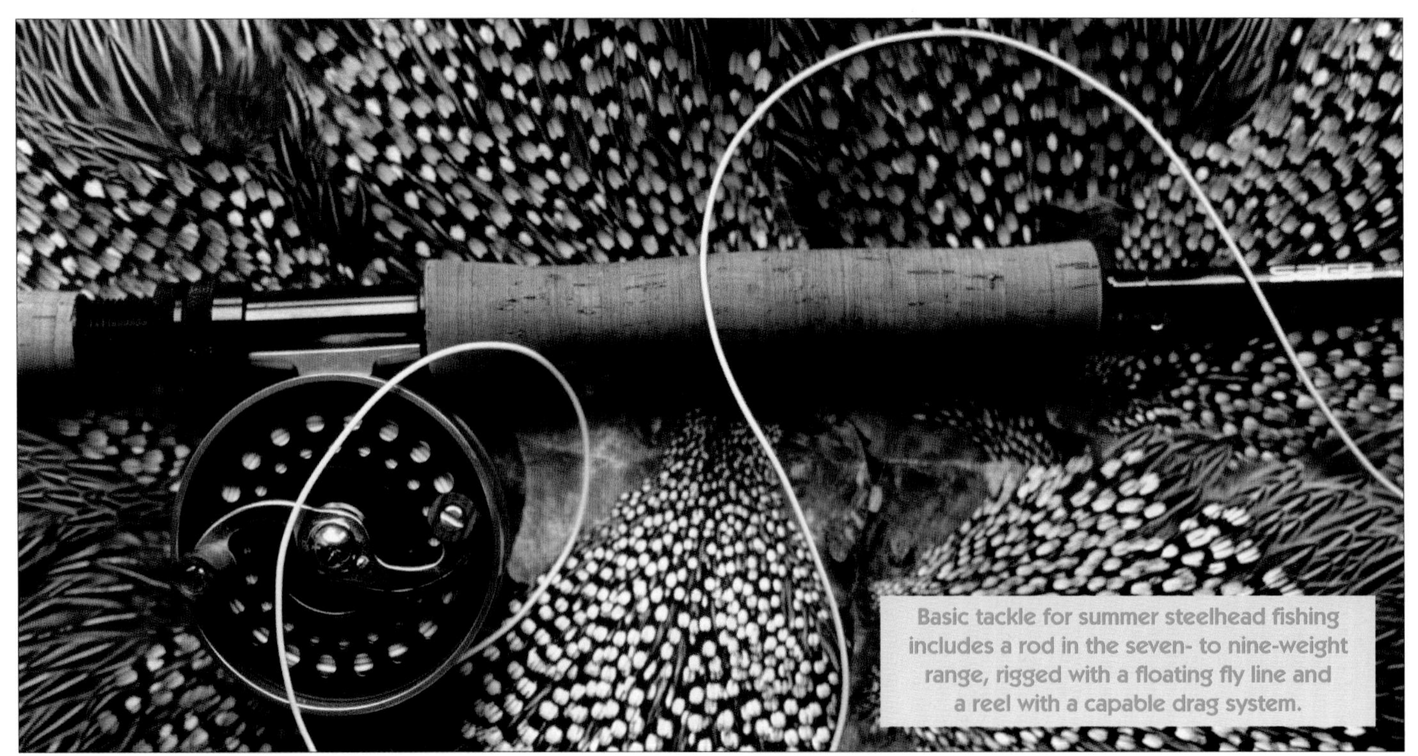

Basic tackle for summer steelhead fishing includes a rod in the seven- to nine-weight range, rigged with a floating fly line and a reel with a capable drag system.

Shooting taper line systems allow for long casts with a minimum of false casting and a minimum of backcast room.

Knots

Attaching Loop to Fly Line

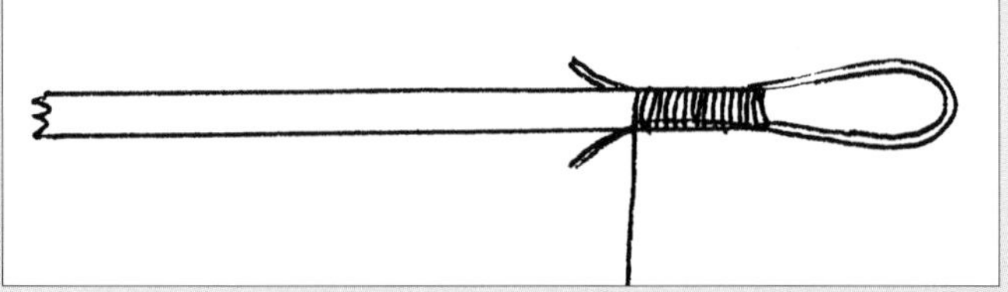

Use Kevlar or Nymo thread to whip a short loop of Dacron backing material to the end of the fly line. After 2 or 3 layers of tight thread wraps, add a coat of Plio Bond or similar finish and allow to dry. Trim ends and test the loop for strength.

Perfection Loop

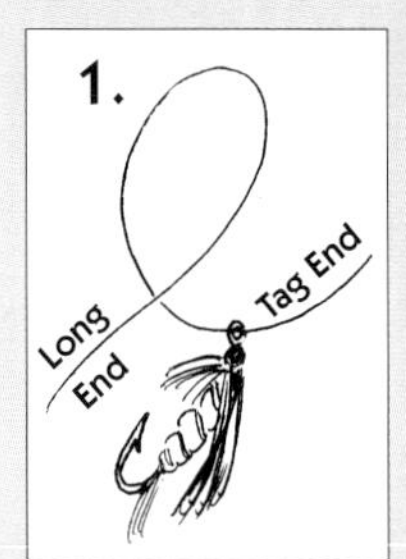

Form a loop of tippet material and then slide the fly over the tag end. Hold the loop and the fly between your left thumb and index finger.

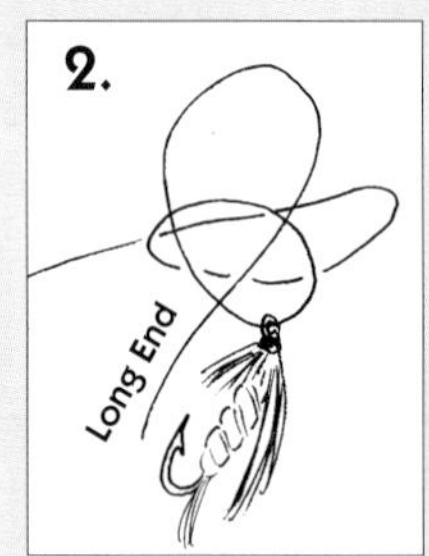

Wrap a second loop around the first by passing the tag end right to left over the front of the first loop and then left to right behind this first loop. Hold the second loop between your thumb and finger and then pass the tag end right to left between the two loops.

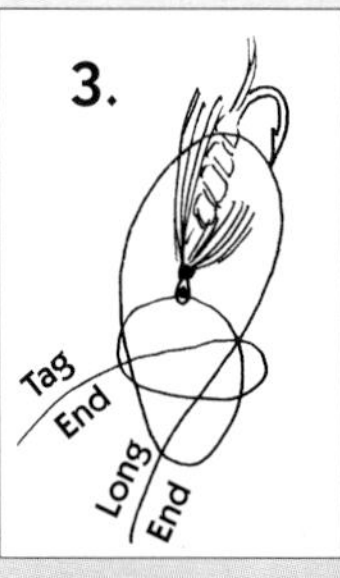

Now shorten the second loop by pulling up on the left side of the first loop. Pass the fly front to back through the first loop.

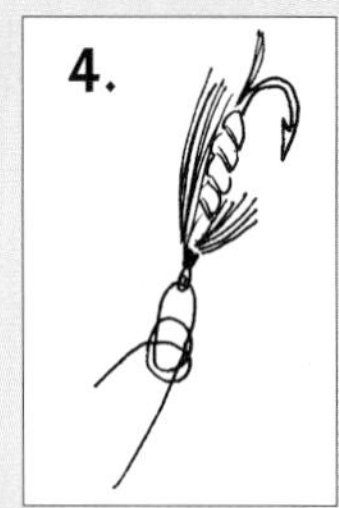

Now pull on the long end of the leader to tighten knot.

The completed perfection loop.

Using a loop knot to attach leader and fly will help prevent the tippet from lassoing the fly. Nonetheless, you should regularly check the fly and the connecting knots.

If you persist in steelhead angling, you will want a good reel to match your favorite rod. We've landed lots of steelhead on gutless reels, but our percentage of fish landed to fish hooked has no doubt increased in proportion to the increasing quality of our reels. A good steelhead reel needs three ingredients: Durability, line capacity and an effective, simple drag system.

Line Systems

Having settled on a reel, you are left with countless line choices. For the vast majority of your summer steelhead fishing, all you need is a floating line. A weight-forward taper is most useful unless you fish small streams or other places where roll casting is at a premium. In that case, double-taper floating lines might be the better choice.

We frequent big rivers, so we fish weight-forward tapers—at least when we fish full fly lines. More often we use shooting tapers or "shooting heads." These shooting tapers are basically nothing more than radical weight-forward designs that you assemble yourself. The floating shooting taper begins with a length of "running line." This running line, usually at least 100 feet long, is a thin diameter material that will shoot through the guides quickly and easily. We use 25- or 30-pound-test monofilament, generally of a brand called Amnesia. This Amnesia material resists kinking and coiling better than most monofilaments.

Next you will need either a factory-made floating shooting taper fly line or a home-made version of the same thing. These lines cost about half or a third the price of a full fly line. If you would prefer to make your own, buy a double-taper fly line that is two line weights heavier than the line designated for your rod. Then cut the front 36 feet or so from this double-taper line and attach this length of line to your running line. Then, following the casting instructions on page 14, see how well it casts. If the line feels awkward, heavy and cumbersome, try chopping a couple feet off at a time until you arrive at a length that casts smoothly (typically 30 feet or so, but this will vary from rod to rod).

During this testing phase, you can use nail knots to attach fly line to running line. After that, you should convert to loops. Tie a perfection loop or other loop knot at the end of the running line. Then attach a loop of Dacron to the back end of the shooting taper (see accompanying instructions for securing a loop to the fly line). With this loop-to-loop system, you can easily change from the floating "head" to an intermediate or sinking head on those few occasions when such a change is warranted.

To the other end of the shooting taper you will attach a leader. We have found leader-shy steelhead to be at best exceedingly rare. Thus we always opt for tippets in the 10- to 15-pound range and leaders that total about nine feet. Despite the popularity of the fu-fu designer tapered leaders available in all the fly shops, we stick with good old Maxima. We've had some bad experiences with the brand-name fly leaders, but take a length of 12-pound-test Maxima and roll it around in the dirt, play tug-o-war with the dog, run over it with the jeep and jump up and down on it and likely it will still test out at about 12 pounds. We say that without any considerations whatsoever from the manufacturers of Maxima—we are just sold on the product.

We use loop knots to attach fly to tippet. An open loop allows the fly to swing freely. More importantly, the tippet will rarely lasso the fly when you use a loop knot. With a clinch knot, you will spend a certain amount of time fishing with a fly that is tangled up in the

Good wading gear coupled with aggressive but intelligent wading allows steelhead anglers to fish places that most folks will pass by. Cleated boots probably offer the single biggest wading advantage to steelhead anglers.

tippet and then usually swimming backward in the water—a position from which the fly cannot hope to hook a steelhead. The perfection loop is easy and fast to tie (see instructions).

Our shooting-taper systems are capable of slightly more distance than many full-length fly lines, but this is not really their primary advantage. More importantly, these "shooting heads" allow us to cover the water more efficiently. Efficient casting leads directly to more fish: The more time your line spends on the water rather than in the air, the more chances you have of drifting the fly in front of a steelhead. In other words, if you can keep false casting to a minimum, your fly will spend a lot more time in the river and you will cover substantially more water during a day.

Moreover, the shooting taper system allows us to change lines quickly and easily when a sinking or sink-tip line might be needed. To make such a change, we need only unloop one shooting taper from the running line and loop on another—no messing around with spare spools and no need to re-string the line through the guides. Certainly some of the new-generation weight-forward fly lines will cast as easily and as far as our shooting tapers, but with any full-length line you must switch spools and re-string the rod when you want to go from one line to another.

Casting the Shooting Taper

During the cast, the shooting taper, or fly-line section of your rig, will never be inside the rod guides. Instead, strip off the running line until somewhere between three and six feet of this mono hangs out the tip-top guide. Peel off an additional 30 or more feet of mono from the reel. Holding the running line in your off hand, cast a smooth, tight loop and then, as the line straightens on the forestroke, release the running line from your hand, allowing it to "shoot" out the guides behind the fly line. The idea is pretty simple: deliver a cast of say, 80 feet, but begin with only half of that in the air, the remainder being carried out by the weight of the shooting taper, much like a spinner or spoon provides the weight to pull mono from a spinning reel.

Now take the whole operation to the river and you can see the efficiency involved: You are waist-deep in a big steelhead run. You deliver an 80-foot cast as described above. The fly completes its swing and you are ready to take a couple steps downstream to cast again. As you take those two or three steps, you are simultaneously stripping in running line until the back end of the fly line is some three to eight feet away from the tip-top guide on the rod. Holding the running line in a couple of big loops, you pick up the shooting taper, which is hanging directly downstream, with a backstroke. Make one false cast to turn the angle of the cast to about 45-degrees down-and-across and then deliver the fly again.

At the completion of each swing, you strip in line as you step downstream and deliver another cast as described above. No monkeying around with three or four false casts. Just cast, swing the fly, step and strip, cast again, swing, step and strip, and so on. You cover the water much faster than would be possible when multiple false casts are involved and you cast long distances with minimal effort.

It is just this efficiency that the new-generation weight-forward lines seek to duplicate. Lines like Lee Wulff's Triangle Taper and the new steelhead and saltwater tapers from Cortland and Scientific Anglers perform in much the same manner. Essentially they are floating shooting tapers that use thin-diameter fly line as running line. Although these thin-diameter running lines shoot through the guides quite effectively, none are as smooth as monofilament. On the other hand, they are somewhat less prone to tangles and they achieve their respective taper designs without the loop-to-loop knots needed for monofilament setups.

Shooting the line, of course, comprises the key component in using a shooting taper system to its fullest advantage. To do so efficiently, you must do three things properly: 1. "load" the rod on the back cast; 2. deliver a smooth, tight loop; 3. release the running line from your free hand at the right time with a minimum of resistance.

Loading the rod for the cast simply means that you are providing enough line weight to flex the rod—this flexing of the rod being what catapults the line through the air. You begin with several feet of running line outside of the tip-top guide, the exact amount of which will vary from line to line. Starting with too much running line outside the guides will cause all kinds of problems in your casting. To achieve a good cast with the shooting tapers that we typically fish, we must leave somewhere between five and ten feet of mono extending beyond the rod tip at the beginning of the cast.

In any case, to load the rod effectively, you must first generate ample line speed on the backcast and then stop the forestroke abruptly. Perhaps the easiest way to do this with a floating shooting taper is to use a "water haul" or "water cast," wherein you begin with a short, straight cast aimed toward your target. On this initial cast, you do not release the running line but instead pick up immediately for a backstroke and then deliver the actual cast. The resistance caused when the line is plucked from the water causes a substantial flex on the ensuing backstroke, thus generating ample line speed to deliver a long cast.

This water haul requires some practice, but otherwise seems to be the most efficient method for generating line speed for a long cast with your floating shooting taper.

The second requirement in casting the shooting taper—the smooth, tight loop on the forestroke—is first a product of a tight loop on the backstroke (generated by the water haul) and secondly a fruition of abruptly checking the forward motion of your rod tip on the forestroke. All the arm strength in the world won't deliver a long cast unless the caster learns to stop the rod tip fairly high in the air, allowing the rod to flex to its full potential.

As you check the forward motion of the rod tip, enabling the rod to flex, you must also release the running line. Release the mono too early and the tight loop comes unglued (and you had

John Shewey with a Deschutes River summer run. Photo by Ken Hanley.

better duck!); release too late and the shooting taper sort of trips over itself and nose dives into the water. Thus precise timing of the release leads to ideal casts. Add to all this the fact that you will be double hauling and the exact moment of release is pretty much second nature for many casters. If you have not yet mastered the double haul, you will want to do so as you learn how to cast the shooting taper.

Two-Handed Rods

Two-handed rods (Spey rods) have become increasingly popular for steelhead angling. Used traditionally on the salmon rivers of Scotland, these rods typically run 13 to 16 feet in length and are designed for "Spey casting." Essentially a dressed up form of roll casting, Spey casting allows you to cover lots of water without the need to backcast. Thus obstacles on the bank behind you are never a concern as they sometimes are in traditional single-handed casting. Moreover, the long rods allow for maximum line-mending ability and hence fly control.

Over the course of your steelheading days, you will no doubt find pools and runs where the two-handed rod and proficiency in its use will offer a distinct advantage over the single-handed rod. Nonetheless, we ourselves persist in the use of our single-handed rods and shooting-taper systems. On those occasions when we fish places that offer no backcasting room, we just switch to full floating fly lines and roll cast. In fact, we at times find ourselves practicing the "double-Spey cast," which is really nothing more than two roll casts executed one right after the other. For specifics on Spey casting, you can look up any of several authors, including Joan Wulff, Hugh Faulkus and Deke Meyer.

Spey rods certainly have their disadvantages: Landing a steelhead is a burdensome affair unless you have a wide, uncluttered beach behind you. Moreover—and one of the reasons we have not been too eager to jump on the Spey-casting bandwagon—a steelhead exerts substantially more leverage against a 16-foot rod than against a 10-foot rod, thus necessitating a proportionately longer fight. The longer you fight a steelhead, the less that fish's chances of survival once released. Thus, if indeed you decide to experiment with the two-handed rods, by all means fight your fish as quickly and efficiently as possible.

Wading Gear

Aggressive wading, at times, leads to more steelhead. This is not to say you should always strive to wade as far and deep into a pool as possible, but steelhead anglers who are willing and able to wade where others won't, give themselves the advantage of fishing places that don't get fished much.

We have a favorite little pool that offers the perfect example. Really nothing more than a narrow slot tight against the far bank, this little run can be effectively fished only from a shallow bar at mid-river. That's the easy part. Getting out to that bar is the problem. We call this place the 50-Percent Hole because half the time we reach that bar standing and the other half we get there by swimming. Wading across the fast chute separating the near bank from the mid-river bar is an adventure in uncertainty. We start high and take big lunging steps down and across. One missed step or unlucky collision with a rock and down you go.

Despite the acrobatics and colorful language involved, we persist in fishing that little slot because it holds steelhead and is passed over by other anglers.

A sharp hook puts more steelhead on the beach. Notice that the angler drags the point of the hook into the grain of the file. A few such strokes on each side of the point will result in a needle-sharp hook.

Our wading gear, however, has a lot to do with our confidence in such situations. We start with neoprene waders on all but the hottest days. More significant are the boots: Some kind of cleats or studs should be considered mandatory for steelhead fishing. They can save your life. You can buy studded soles for your wading boots or you can opt for any number of different strap-on cleats. For a cheap and simple solution, just buy some 1/2-inch or 5/8-inch sheet-metal screws and screw them into the bottom of your boots (from the outside so the head of the screw becomes the cleat). Place 12 or 15 of these in each sole and you're in business.

Incidentals

Being a rather uncomplicated form of fly fishing, steelheading should likewise be an uncluttered affair. Leave the vest in the truck whenever possible and just carry in your pockets those few things you need: A few extra flies, spool of tippet material, extra leader, extra shooting tapers, nippers, small pliers, hook hone, etc. Certainly you needn't carry two or three fly boxes. Opt instead for a single small box or fly wallet.

Because steelheading can keep you on the river until well after sunset, consider carrying a small flashlight. We've been promising ourselves we would do likewise for years, but we seem to prefer the unpredictable nature of those stumbling, bumbling late-night treks across the river and back to the truck.

No matter what the weather does, always wear a hat and glasses. A No. 2 steelhead fly has a mind of its own when accompanied by a gust of wind and despite the inherent entertainment value for your fellow anglers, the fun is definitely over when you get a Purple Matuka in the scalp or a Brad's Brat in the ear.

Chapter 3

Flies For Summer Steelhead

If we were to assemble one each of every steelhead fly in print today, we would be left with a pile of thousands. Most of these flies, at one time or another, have taken a steelhead for someone somewhere. A few patterns from that pile, however, would be responsible for countless hookups over the years.

Old favorites like the Green-Butt Skunk, Fall Favorite, Purple Peril and Skykomish Sunrise have taken thousands of fish. Is this fact a function of the relative effectiveness of these flies or simply the natural result of so many anglers fishing them? As a general statement, we would argue in favor of the latter—after all, if 100 anglers fish one pattern while one angler fishes a different pattern, we would certainly expect the 100 to hook more fish.

Still, some flies fish better than others: We would choose a simple hairwing skunk long before tying on a fanciful Victorian-style Atlantic salmon fly because our collective experience suggests a basic dark hairwing fly is simply more effective more often than the gaudy, intricate feather wings that have traveled cross-continent to gain a small following amongst steelhead tiers.

Once in a great while the steelhead gods grant an angler the chance to watch how a fish reacts to the fly: You watch your fly swing through the steelhead's window and then watch as the fish moves for the fly, stays put or at times seems to shy away. If the fish fails to move for the fly, you might opt to switch patterns and try again. Sometimes the new fly makes all the difference and we have no idea why. More often, a fish that refuses to move for the first fly, likely won't move for any successive casts. Still, angler's have documented enough of these cases that we can say with some certainty that at times fly choice does make a difference.

We submit, however, that unless you are indeed casting to a visible fish, changing flies offers no advantage. In other words, fly choice matters but the steelheading community has no idea why. Unless we can watch a particular steelhead's reaction to our flies, we simply do not have enough information on which to logically base a decision to change flies. We hardly know why a steelhead takes a fly to begin with so how can we hope to know what factors motivate a fish to choose one pattern and reject another? We can guess, but we simply don't have enough information to form anything but a guess. Thus we feel that a major strategical advantage is gained by the angler who chooses one or two favorite flies from amongst the thousands and then covers the water as diligently and efficiently as possible.

We are often reminded of the many times over the seasons that some elated trout angler has rushed into the shop wide-eyed with a story of how a steelhead jumped all over his No. 12 Elk Hair Caddis or Hare's Ear Nymph. We once fished for a week without moving a steelhead only to have two such trout anglers come running into the shop to tell their respective stories of steelhead pouncing on their trout flies. Why should this happen? We don't know. The biologists don't know. The entire steelheading community doesn't know. It is enough for us that these majestic gamefish will humor us on occasion by grabbing our flies.

In fact, a quick study of the endless horde of steelhead patterns in print today leads to two important conclusions: First, some talented fly tiers have lent their interest to steelhead flies with little regard to steelhead fishing. While this development is certainly to the betterment of the tier's art, it is rather disserving to the beginning steelhead angler who understandably finds tremendous difficulty in choosing a few good flies in which to place his or her confidence and fortunes astream.

Second and more importantly, this vast confusion of patterns suggests that steelhead will grab just about anything at one time or another.

Given both of those facts, how is the beginning steelheader to choose a fly in which to place his or her fate and trust? We grappled with this problem for quite some time before the obvious solution finally emerged from the carnage of our minds. Why not just follow the same ploy we always used while working in the fly shops? A customer walks in and asks what fly we recommend for the North Santiam or the Umpqua or the McKenzie or just about any other river. We escort the customer over to the fly bins, pull out a Purple Matuka and leave it at that. We always sold the flies that we ourselves fished.

An overwhelming majority of the time—probably along the lines of 95 percent of the time—we fish our favorite purple flies, the Purple Matuka and the Spawning Purple. The remaining five percent of the time might see us choose a Brad's Brat or a skunk. That five percent generally involves trips to rivers where we have chosen some favorite river-specific flies. Oregon's Deschutes is the best example of this. Here we might fish a Rick's Revenge or a Mack's Canyon—just for variety if nothing else since the Purple Matuka and Spawning Purple take just as many fish there.

We have developed so much confidence in our favorite flies that on those days when no steelhead is forthcoming, we simply disdain any belief that our flies were the cause of our failure to hook a fish. We go on fishing the Purple Matuka or Spawning Purple with utter confidence. The fly is the absolute last factor on which we will blame a fishless day.

And the fly is the least of our worries once secured to the tippet. That fly will catch fish. Absolutely. Without question. The same confidence that permeates your every cast must extend right down to individual tackle items, especially the fly. In the words of a tele-

The Spawning Purple (top) and the Maxwell's Purple Matuka are the favorite steelhead flies of the authors.

vangelist, "if you want to be healed brother, then you gotta believe," and healed in this game means a chrome-bright summer steelhead trying to yank the rod out of your hand. So tie on a Purple Matuka or a Spawning Purple and be healed. If you choose any other fly, do so with the same utter confidence. The fly you choose will catch fish. Period.

If the Purple Matuka or Spawning Purple don't turn your crank, then opt for one of the 12 other flies listed here. All are dependable, effective flies that, over the years, have taken many steelhead for many anglers. If given a fly from this list and told to go fishing, we would fish any of them with confidence. At the risk of being redundant, we will again point out that countless other flies might prove equal to the task—the 12 in our short list have survived the test of time and have earned our confidence.

If you don't tie your own flies, then finding our two favorites may pose a problem. The Spawning Purple and the Purple Matuka, despite their effectiveness for us, are not in especially widespread use simply because they evolved for us as local patterns without a lot of fanfare. Many fly shops, however, are happy to tie custom orders. Just show them a copy of this book and ask to have a few Spawning Purple's and Purple Matuka's tied up. If you do tie your own flies (and we recommend that every angler begin doing so at some point), you will find steelhead flies to be a relatively easy and thoroughly enjoyable undertaking.

On most rivers, we fish our favorite flies on No. 1/0 through 4 hooks, with No. 2's being our choice most of the time. Some rivers have a reputation for small flies; other for large flies. We've fished such places and always found our No. 2's to catch steelhead.

Naturally, you do have one more option for choosing a fly: If you are headed to a particular river, just ask somebody what flies to use. The local fly shop, fly fishing guides, fly fishing friends or other sources can lead you in the right direction.

Whether you choose one of our favorite flies or one from our short list, or whether you choose a fly based on advice from others, fish that fly with complete confidence.

Top 12 Steelhead Flies

12 Proven Steelhead Flies

1. Skunk
2. Green-Butt Skunk
3. Brad's Brat
4. Mack's Canyon
5. Purple Peril
6. Silver Hilton
7. Thor
8. Del Cooper
9. Skykomish Sunrise
10. Orange Heron
11. Cumming's Special
12. Rick's Revenge

Fly Style

Ask five different tiers to whip up a Green-Butt Skunk and you might well get five rather different flies. Although the elements that identify the flies as Green-Butt Skunks remain (black body, green butt, black hackle, red tail, white wing), different tiers often choose different materials, methods and proportions to arrive at the same pattern.

Don't let these differences in style bother you too much when you buy flies. Steelhead really don't care much about style: We would fish a chenille-body fly with every bit as much confidence as a dubbed-body pattern. We prefer to tie the latter simply because the style pleases our sense of aesthetics. So long as it functions properly (e.g. remain submerged when they're supposed to and hook fish solidly), a fly's style is largely irrelevant to the angler who fishes with confidence.

Perhaps the perfect example of differences in style can be seen in what we call "low-water flies." Designed to appear smaller and less obtrusive to spooky fish holding in low, clear summer flows, low-water flies are tied in a "reduced" fashion. The best way to describe a low-water dressing is to simply imagine a No. 8 fly tied on a No. 4 hook. In our experience, we have never proven a low-water fly to make any difference to the steelhead. The important issue, as always, is that if an angler enjoys fishing low-water flies and fishes them with confidence, he or she will catch fish. That thought transcends fly style: Tie your flies in whatever style pleases you and then simply fish them without a second thought.

Photographed here are four different styles of the same fly (a Brad's Brat). All share the same color scheme that identifies them as Brad's Brats, but all display a different style arrived at through different materials, proportions, tying methods and interpretations. This is the real beauty of tying steelhead flies: You can explore different styles, tie your own way, and still expect to catch fish. Indeed,

Fly Style: By applying different materials, techniques and interpretations, we can devise different "styles" of the same pattern, in this case a Brad's Brat. Pictured here are a Brad's Brat featherwing and Brad's Brat Matuka tied by Forrest Maxwell (top) and a standard hairwing Brad's Brat and Spey-style Brad's Brat tied by John Shewey.

this is one reason why we disdain the use of some of today's so-called steelhead flies—Lead-Head Bunny Leeches, Articulated Leeches, Girdle Bugs and egg flies. After all, given the chance to catch a steelhead on a beautifully crafted classic-style steelhead fly, why would anyone choose not to do so?

Indeed, when crafting your steelhead flies, you will have numerous choices in terms of materials. To help guide you on your way in this wondrous art, we have compiled a list of materials that can be used to create the various parts of the fly.

Tags: tinsel, usually flat or fine oval; sometimes a few turns of floss or a combination of tinsel and floss

Tails: hackle fibers, golden pheasant crest or tippets (dyed or natural), calftail, bucktail, polar bear or its substitutes, floss strands, marabou, duck flank, deer hair, etc.

Ribs: usually tinsel (flat, oval or embossed), sometimes floss, wire or synthetics like Krystal Flash

Bodies: chenille, wool, yarn, floss, silk, dubbed fur (seal or angora, rabbit, etc.), dyed ostrich, tinsel, combinations thereof

Hackles: rooster neck and saddle hackles (often dyed), hen hackles, golden pheasant and ringneck pheasant feathers, duck flank, dyed duck flank, guinea fowl, etc.

Wings: calftail, bucktail, polar bear, skunk, fox, squirrel tail, goat, calf body hair, fitch tail, marabou, hackle tips, bronze mallard, duck flank, golden pheasant plumage, and many others

Dressings

Skunk

Tag: Silver
Tail: Red
Body: Black
Rib: Silver
Hackle: Black
Wing: White or black (or white over black)
Variations: Add fluorescent green butt for Green-Butt Skunk, fluorescent red butt for Red-Butt Skunk.

Brad's Brat (originated by Enos Bradner)

Tag: Gold
Tail: Orange
Body: Rear part orange, front part red (usually the rear 1/3 to 2/5 is orange, the remainder being red)
Rib: Gold
Hackle: Brown, dark furnace or mottled brown
Wing: White with orange over the top

Mack's Canyon (originated by Doug Stewart)

Tag: Gold
Tail: Orange or orange and white
Rib: Gold
Body: Rear half orange, front half black
Hackle: Black
Wing: White with orange over top

Purple Peril (originated by Ken McLeod)

Tag: Silver
Tail: Purple
Rib: Silver
Body: Purple
Hackle: Purple
Wing: Dark (brown squirrel, brown bear or similar)

Silver Hilton

Tag: Silver
Tail: Teal or pintail flank
Rib: Silver
Body: Black
Wing: Grizzly hackle feathers
Hackle: Grizzly or duck flank (teal, pintail, mallard, etc.)
Variations: Add fluorescent green butt for Green-Butt Silver Hilton; purple body and flame orange butt for Purple Flame Hilton.

Thor (originated by C. Jim Pray)

Tag: Gold or none
Tail: Orange or brown
Body: Red
Hackle: Brown
Wing: White

Del Cooper (originated by Mike Kennedy)

Tag: Silver
Tail: Red
Body: Purple
Rib: Silver
Hackle: Purple
Wing: White

Skykomish (originated by George McLeod)

Tag: Silver or none
Tail: Red and yellow hackle fibers mixed, or red-dyed and natural golden pheasant crest
Rib: Silver

Body: Bright red
Hackle: Mix of yellow and red
Wing: White

Orange Heron (originated by Syd Glasso)

Tag: Silver or none
Body: 2/3 orange silk or floss; front third orange Angora dubbing or similar
Rib: Medium or wide flat silver tinsel trailed on the rear edge by fine silver oval
Hackle: Blue-eared pheasant rump hackle following path of ribs through body
Throat: Teal flank
Wing: Four orange saddle or neck hackle tips

Cumming's Special (originated by Ward Cummings and Clarence Gordon)

Body: 1/3 yellow-orange silk, floss or wool, 2/3 claret wool, dubbing or chenille
Rib: Gold
Hackle: Claret
Wing: Brown (bucktail, squirrel or brown bear)

Rick's Revenge (originated by John Shewey)

Tag: Silver flat tinsel
Tail: Hot pink or hot orange floss
Butt: Hot pink or hot orange floss (1/3 or 2/5 total body length)
Body: Purple
Rib: Fine silver or gold oval
Hackle: Purple
Wing: White topped with purple
Throat: Purple-dyed guinea or teal

Tying Maxwell's Purple Matuka

Hook: No. 4/0-6, steelhead wet fly
Tag: Flat silver tinsel
Rib: Medium silver oval tinsel
Body: Black (dubbed Angora fur; wool; chenille; etc.)
Wing: Two or four purple hackles, tied matuka style
Collar: Purple hackle

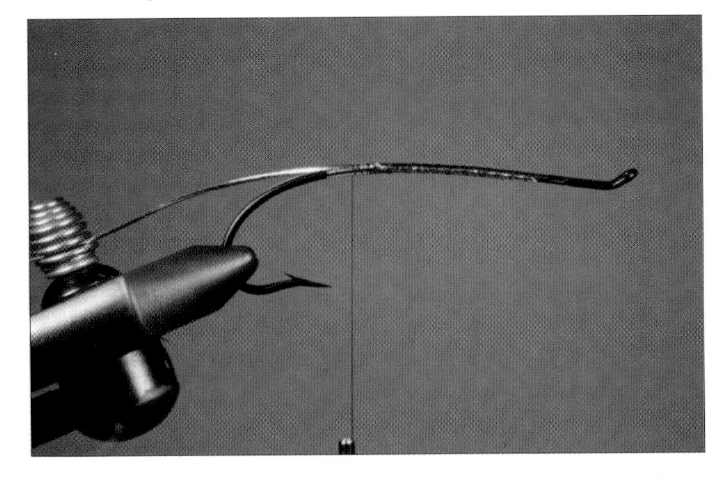

Step 1. Secure the tag as follows: Attach a length of fine flat silver tinsel about 2/3 down the shank. Wrap this tinsel backward, keeping each wrap tight against the previous one but without overlapping the wraps. At a point opposite the point or barb of the hook, reverse direction and begin wrapping the tinsel back up the shank, again making sure each turn of tinsel lays tight against the previous wrap but without overlapping. Tie off the tinsel near the starting point. Wind the thread forward and secure a length of fine or medium silver oval along the hook shank.

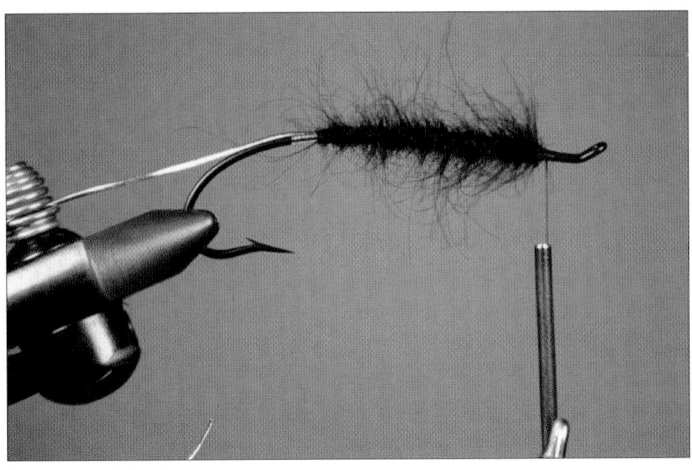

Step 2. Now form a body of black dubbed fur, wool or similar (we prefer black Angora goat dubbing), leaving at the rear a short tag of the flat silver tinsel.

Step 3. At the front of the body, secure back-to-back purple hackle feathers, shiny sides facing outward. Tie these in securely so they cannot pull out as you rib the fly.

Step 4. Stroke the hackle fibers upward with one hand while holding the stems down against the fly with the other. Once the hackle fibers are standing up at right angles to the stem, you can begin binding the feathers down by spiraling the silver oval over the body of the fly.

Step 5. Having completed this rib in about six turns, add a collar of purple hackle at the front. Tie off and cement the head.

Tying The Spawning Purple

Thread: Fluorescent flame-orange single-strand floss and then orange or black 6/0 or smaller thread
Hook: No. 3/0-6, salmon/steelhead wet fly
Tag: Silver flat tinsel
Body: Flame orange single-strand floss (used as tying thread)
Wing: Four or five separate "spikes" of purple marabou tied in at intervals along the top of the hook, beginning at about mid-shank; the last of these is tied in after the purple hackle is wrapped
Collar: Purple hackle
Cheeks: Jungle cock (optional)
Second Collar: Dyed-orange guinea

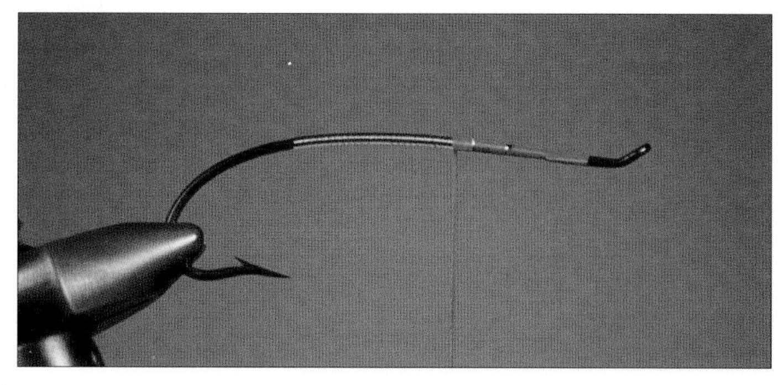

Step 1. Secure a length of fine flat silver tinsel just ahead of mid-shank. Wrap this tinsel backward and then forward again in the manner described for the Purple Matuka, thus forming both the tag and a silver underbody.

Step 2. Wrap backward with the single-strand floss, forming a thin butt. Leaving a turn or two of silver tinsel showing for a tag, reverse direction with the floss and wrap back to mid-shank. At this point, secure a wing of purple marabou fibers (use the entire tip section from a marabou "blood plume"). This "spike" of marabou, when pulled to the rear, should extend to the back of the hook bend.

Step 3. Tie in three more of these marabou spikes, leaving a gap between the respective tie-down points. Each successive spike must be cut slightly longer than the previous ones so that the ends are even at the rear.

Step 4. After securing the fourth spike of marabou, switch to the fine thread and secure a purple hackle. Make five or six turns of hackle for a collar.

Step 5. Now add a fifth spike of purple marabou and then, if desired, add a long jungle cock eye to each side of the wing. Then finish the fly by making two or three turns of orange-dyed guinea (use the long-fibered rump feathers for large flies).

Some places, no matter how small or inaccessible, simply look too good not to receive a few casts. As you spend more and more time on the steelhead rivers, you will begin to develop an intuitive sense that tells you to stop and take a few casts in certain places that might not otherwise fit the classic definition of a steelhead pool.

Chapter 4

The Wet-Fly Swing

No its not the name of the latest dance down at the local grange hall, but like a timeless waltz, the wet-fly swing has endured the ages, arriving in steelhead-dom by way of the Atlantic salmon literature of the last century. The wet-fly swing is the method around which this book is built. It is the classic steelheading technique and as effective today as it was during the infancy of our sport.

What's more, the wet-fly swing is simple to learn and easy to practice. Given the simplicity of this basic steelhead fly fishing technique, we find it both amazing and unfortunate that the sport is surrounded by a shroud of mystery that says to the beginner that he or she has very little chance of success without first becoming a wizard with the rod and a master of the river.

Indeed, it is the wet-fly swing that gives every angler the chance to become both of these things to one extent or another. No other steelheading technique brings you so close to the river. This classic method of steelhead fly fishing, by its very design, dictates that you immerse yourself, so to speak, in the characteristics of the river around you. No other method allows you to so thoroughly cover the water and as such, no other method can teach you as much about steelhead and where they will rest in any given piece of water. Lastly, no other method—no other opportunity in all of fly fishing save the closely related art of Atlantic salmon fishing—teaches you to cast and wade like the classic wet-fly swing.

As trout anglers we spend our entire lives dedicated to the elimination of drag in the presentation of a drifting fly. With the wet-fly swing method of steelhead fishing, however, we use drag to our advantage. More than that, we want the fly to drag, to swing across the river in a slow, controlled arc.

Cast down and across stream at an approximate 45-degree angle. Mend the line to straighten the leader and sink the fly, then allow the line to come tight under tension from the currents. As it does so, the fly begins to swing back to your side of the river. That's the wet-fly swing in a nutshell. Cast, mend, swing. Simple.

The wet-fly swing is so simple in design that even in slightly practiced hands its application is artistic. The wet-fly swing is methodical to the degree that casting down and across and swinging the fly cross current over and over while wading down through a steelhead run gathers a rhythm of its own, a rhythm that seems to belong there on the river with the fragrant conifers and the vibrant maples; the bobbing water ouzels and the dancing caddisflies; the misty dawns and the enveloping dusks. Through it all the river whispers along and the fly line swishes to and fro in harmony.

Indeed the wet-fly swing is grace and poetry. It is easy to learn and its practitioner is intimately connected to the river. More than that, this method is effective. Rarely in fly fishing, in fact, can we expect such overwhelming results from such a simple technique: Just learn to read steelhead water, apply the wet-fly swing and you will catch steelhead.

Sometimes called a "quartering cast," this down-and-across cast that begins the wet-fly swing places the fly above the water you intend to fish and some distance across from your position. Imagine a straight line running down the middle of the river. A perpendicular line cuts off 90-degree angles. Place a 45-degree angle going down and away from your position. This is the direction you will cast.

Make your first cast at the upstream end of the pool or run you are fishing. Begin with short casts, but with each successive presentation, lengthen the line some five or six feet. When you have extended the cast to a length of line that you can handle efficiently, you can stop stripping line off the reel. From this point on you will move downriver in one-, two- or three-step increments after each presentation.

The decision to move one, two or three steps between casts is primarily dictated by the depth of the water in the particular run you are fishing. In shallow water the effective vision of a steelhead (or any fish for that matter) is greatly reduced. Conversely, a steelhead holding in deep water necessarily views a proportionately larger area. Since the basic purpose of the wet-fly swing is to present the fly to every available fish in the pool, a shorter distance between presentations in shallow water will assure that each fish receives at least one opportunity to see the fly. Similarly, water that is slightly colored might encourage you to reduce the distance between presentations to assure thorough coverage of the pool.

Often, in fact, we will decide to make only a single step between casts based on a gut feeling that a particular pool or run feels "fishy." That's a tough one to explain, but as your steelheading experience mounts you will most certainly begin to understand and listen to that inner voice that tells you to "fish this pool thoroughly."

Sometimes you will see one or more steelhead holding in the pool you intend to fish. These situations also warrant a shorter distance between casts, but don't dwell too long on non-biters. Many steelhead that you will encounter simply will not move for the fly. Remember, we are after those fish that are inclined to oblige our efforts by chasing the fly and to find these aggressive individuals, we must present our fly to as many steelhead as possible during the day. Certainly you should offer some extra casts to sighted fish, perhaps even changing flies in an attempt to get their attention, but once you've expended what seems like a reasonable amount of effort, move on to other fish.

In any event, the entire presentation works as follows: After casting your measured amount of line down and across you will

Down-and-Across Wet-Fly Swing

Executing the down-and-across wet-fly swing: The angler delivers a down-and-across cast that places the fly at the far side of the pool (A and B). A short drag-free drift (C) allows the fly to sink a few inches before coming under tension from the taut line (D). From this particular location in this pool, no further mending is needed to affect the slow cross-current swing—we call such pools "self-menders." The angler simply allows the fly to swing across the pool (E and F).

Water Level View of Down-and-Across Wet-Fly Swing

The angler delivers the down-and-across cast (A), but then must mend immediately upstream to set up the swing (B) before

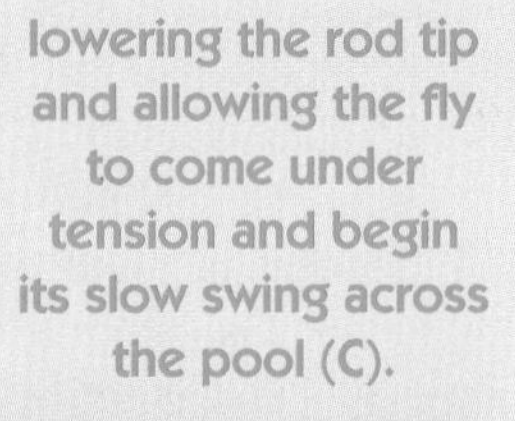

lowering the rod tip and allowing the fly to come under tension and begin its slow swing across the pool (C).

immediately mend the line upstream, an act which straightens the leader and also allows for the fly to sink a few inches before coming under tension. After the fly dead drifts a few feet, it suddenly comes to life as the line pulls tight in the currents. In some pools, the ones we call "self-menders," you need do nothing else. Just allow the fly to swing all the way through until it hangs directly downstream from you. Then take one, two or three steps downstream and repeat the procedure with the same amount of line.

Many pools require you to mend during the swing. The goal of virtually any mend you make will be to control the speed of the fly. A fly that whips across river too fast gives steelhead very little time to react. No rules exist for precise fly speed—just make whatever mends are needed to allow the fly to swing reasonably slowly through the pool. Typically, these mends will be to the upstream side of the fly; sometimes a downstream mend is needed to guide the fly through dead spots or current seams.

Cast, mend, swing the fly and then take two steps downriver. Cast again; mend and swing the fly again. Take another two steps downriver and repeat the sequence. Continue in this manner until you have covered the pool or run. Remember, you are searching for the aggressive steelhead, the steelhead willing to leave the comfort of his holding lie and chase your fly. The more water you cover, the more chances you have of presenting the fly to aggressive fish.

Rod Position for Controlling the Speed and Position of the Swinging Fly

Rod position can be critical in controlling the speed and position of the swinging fly. Here the angler casts to a prime-looking slot (A). Notice, however, that because of the deep water the angler cannot wade far enough out on the gravel bar to put himself in the ideal position to control the swing of the fly. To compensate, he simply reaches the rod toward mid-river, thus slowing the fly as it swings through the pool (B). As the fly reaches the middle of the run, the angler gradually swings the rod tip downriver to further reduce the speed of the fly.

To that end, you should learn to cover the water efficiently. Minimize false casting between presentations and train yourself to strip in line in preparation for the next cast as you are taking those two or three steps downstream. Steelhead fly fishing in this classic style builds rapidly on itself: The more time you spend casting and wading, the better you become at both. After all, no better casting practice exists than getting out on a steelhead stream that demands your best efforts.

Not only will your casting improve because of the wet-fly swing, but your ability to read water will improve throughout your steelheading days. As you hook more and more steelhead, you will begin to recognize subtle differences in the flow and character of the river that dictate why a fish will hold in one place and not another. As you progress as a steelhead angler, you will learn to instinctively recognize those parts of the river most likely to hold fish. You will cease to be surprised when you hook a fish in a place that looks ideal or even marginal; instead you will stand slack-jawed in disbelief every time you fish through ideal water without touching a fish. But the latter will not affect your confidence, for the more time you spend astream, covering the water with quartering casts and wading through pools and runs of all varieties, the greater will grow your belief that a steelhead is forthcoming on the next cast—no matter how many casts you've already made that day.

The Take

Nothing else in fly fishing can imitate that precious, brief instant when a steelhead grabs your swinging fly. One moment you are watching the line progress slowly across the river. You know the fly's general location and orientation, so you picture the way it is swimming cross current, undulating and dancing under tension from the line. You are relaxed, yet you anticipate the fish—the pool, the river itself, simply looks too good not to produce a steelhead.

The first hints of autumn have painted a few maple leaves, whose unwavering tranquility intimates the perfect morning weather. A few caddisflies linger over the river, occasionally being assaulted from below by an eager trout. A brace of mergansers zips upriver and you marvel at the water ouzel as it disappears momentarily under a rushing riffle in the shallows, only to bob back to the surface perfectly dry, flitter to the nearest moss-covered rock and announce its presence with its wondrously melodious song.

Just then it happens. Suddenly, but not as if rushed. The line is tight and it is heavy. The fish is on. It feels the taut line as you do and rushes madly downriver. The battle is on and you will probably beach this fish. But the most precious moment of all has been relished already and will be stowed away in the confines of your mind to be cherished through the years—that moment you feel the weight of a steelhead on the end of your line. The moment of the take.

Indeed, the wet-fly swing by definition means that the steelhead will take the fly on a taut line. Thus not only do you feel the weight and the strength of the fish immediately, but you can also be reasonably assured of good hookups. In fact, the best way to hook a steelhead on a taut line is to simply do nothing at all. Assuming you are fishing the line directly from the reel, your reel's drag setting, a sharp hook and a strong tippet will combine with the taut line to drive the hook home.

Then the fight is on. Use your reel's drag system and use the leverage of a strong rod. Give the fish its head when it runs, then work it when it stops; give in to its ensuing runs, allowing the reel's drag to tire it. When it jumps, point the rod toward it. As the fish tires, try to turn it in directions it would rather not go. Steer it clear of rocks and ledges; move downriver or upriver as needed. Work it toward the bank, where it can be most easily cradled. If it is a wild fish, slip the hook from its jaw, revive it if needed and watch the fish glide back into the depths. If it is a hatchery fish and you wish to kill and eat it, you have that right where such action is allowed. Kill the fish quickly with a sharp blow to the head, then barbecue or bake it that night or the next. Or you may simply choose to release all steelhead, allowing them a chance to thrill another fly angler as they have thrilled you.

Setting Up the Wet-Fly Swing, Water-Level View

The angler casts down and across (A and B) and then immediately mends line upstream (C), allowing the fly to dead drift momentarily before beginning its swing (D).

Chapter 5

Reading Steelhead Water

Pools. Runs. Slots. Tailouts, Chutes. Holding water. Resting water. The terms attached to parts of a steelhead river can be endlessly confusing. During our combined 20-plus years working in fly shops, we explored countless ways of trying to tell people how to read steelhead water.

Eventually we found a way around most of the confusion. When asked what constituted steelhead water, we began responding this way: "Look for water between your knees and your eyebrows, maybe a little deeper, and flowing at about the speed you can walk."

Naturally, such a description covers a lot of ground in the average steelhead river, but steelhead do indeed occupy many places in the typical stream. They stop and linger for a time at certain places in the river. Traditional views tell us that steelhead linger at these places, these "holding lies," in order to rest after negotiating a section of river during their upstream migration. The fact that we often find steelhead holding above rapids, long riffles and water falls perhaps offers evidence for the widely held traditional beliefs about steelhead behavior. In reality, we can't prove why steelhead linger at certain places along their routes, but nonetheless they do so. In fact, the key to reading steelhead water lies simply in learning to recognize those places where a steelhead will stop and hold for a time.

Understanding another basic fact about steelhead migration is paramount to our methods and success as well: Steelhead wander into the rivers in small schools and packs, quickly dividing into smaller groups and individuals as they leave tidewater and head for the upper reaches of the river. In other words, they don't invade the rivers all at once in big schools. Therefore, you might find a pool devoid of steelhead one day but holding several fresh arrivals the next day and then holding only a single fish another day. Day in and day out, throughout the summer season, the pools will hold steelhead, whether a single fish or 20 individuals.

In any case, these terms "pool" and "run" that are tossed about freely in steelhead literature simply refer to the places where steelhead stop and where anglers search for them. Both words can be used interchangably, although a pool in the classic sense has distinct parts: the "head," where the rapids or riffle above feeds the pool; the "throat" or "body" of the pool where the water slows to a more deliberate pace and where the river deepens; the "tailout" or "tail" at the downstream end where the river fans out and shallows.

A "run," unlike a pool, does not exhibit such easily distinguished parts. Take the throat of a pool, stick it somewhere else on

While not as easy to read as a typical steelhead pool, this section of river clearly offers several fishable spots, the best of which are the small slots just above the white water on the right side and the tailout just above the grass-covered rock at mid-river a few yards below. The slot between these two places sometimes holds a fish as well.

Fishing the head of the pool: Here the angler fishes the shallow, choppy riffle water at the top of a long pool. Many anglers pass by the productive water at the head of a pool.

the river without its clearly defined head and tailout and you have a run. A run may be little more than a slightly deeper chute or a well-defined slot through an otherwise shallow expanse of riffle water. Such places often hold fish.

Steelhead prefer certain spots in any given run or pool. Year in and year out they will stop and hold at these specific places. These "holding lies" offer some protection from the full brunt of the current, but being big, strong fish, steelhead don't need much help against the river's flow. We've seen steelhead holding behind a single rock no bigger than a grapefruit, beside rock ledges only inches higher than the surrounding streambed, in the most shallow of depressions and along gravel bars that slope just enough to deflect the current ever so slightly.

More commonly, steelhead will hold above, beside and well below large rocks. Given a choice they seem to avoid areas of swirling backeddies, which is why steelhead don't seem overly inclined to hold immediately behind a large protruding rock as trout are prone to do. The current seam trailing down both sides of such rocks is fair game, however, and steelhead often occupy these places. They also hold along ledges and bedrock rifts and in depressions cut into bedrock, cobblestone or gravel bottoms. They avoid the "frogwater" (the barely-moving backwaters and edges home to baby fish and frogs) and prefer the pools and runs over smaller holding places amidst expansive riffles. Nonetheless, many riffles feature small runs—nothing more than deeper troughs and miniature tailouts, but places where a steelhead might stop and hold for a time. So read the riffles carefully and fish anything that might have potential.

Big rivers like the Deschutes can be difficult to read simply because a single pool might span half a mile in length. Nonetheless, if you watch the river carefully, you can pick out slots and runs like this one that offer appropriate depth, ideal current speed and enough cover to deflect the current for holding fish.

Many steelhead pools offer very readable water, such as the throat of this pool on an Oregon river.

Forrest Maxwell hooked a fish on his very last cast in the tailout of this quiet pool—evidence that one should diligently cover all the productive-looking water in any given pool or run.

The body or throat of a large pool like this one may take more than an hour to fish through because the fly swings slowly and the angler may have to cover several hundred yards of productive water.

A classic steelhead pool on the North Umpqua: Looking up from the tailout immediately in front, we can clearly see how the current enters way up at the head of the pool and then fans out through the throat before yielding to the quiet, smooth tailout.

August on a beautiful summer steelhead pool.

A tailout such as this one should be fished all the way to the "lip current" pictured in the foreground, where the water begins to spill over the rocks into the fast water below. Steelhead often hold just above such rocks and the angler who exits the pool before casting to the lip current makes a decided mistake.

Sometimes steelhead hold in surprisingly shallow water and in highly exposed areas. The best way to find these places—in fact the best way to find any holding area—is to cover lots of fishy-looking water with the down-and-across wet-fly swing. As we have said previously, no other method puts you in such intimate quarters with the river.

Alas, when you hook a steelhead, remember that place. You will likely catch more fish there on subsequent days and during years ahead.

Some rivers gain legendary status in part because of their predictability: Steelhead occupy the same lies in the same runs and pools for decades on end. As the seasons come and go, countless fish are taken from these places. The North Umpqua, for example, boasts of its "camp water" near Steamboat where generations of anglers have taken thousands of steelhead from the same holding lies in the same pools and runs. The rocks are scarred from decades of wading cleats striking the same path down through the pools.

Whether a storied river like the North Umpqua or a lesser-known stream, this pattern is typical. Steelhead occupy the same holding lies year in and year out. Whatever attracts one fish to a particular lie obviously appeals to future arrivals as well. Naturally, the better you know a given river, the more of these proven lies you can fish.

Some anglers are content to spend their days fishing well-known pools and holding lies. Others like to explore new water. After all, every river, no matter how famous, hides a few steelhead haunts that are not widely known—a slot here, a little depression there, where once in a while some exploring angler brings a fish to the fly.

In this pool, steelhead tend to hold in the area where the shallow gravel/cobblestone bottom yields to the deeper water near the center.

We employ both strategies. We fish known pools and runs on our favorite rivers, but we are constantly looking for new places where a few exploratory casts might pay dividends. These are the "instinct places," the water that just looks too good not to hold a fish.

A few of our large rivers appear almost featureless when compared to the typical steelhead stream. The lower Deschutes and parts of the Snake are prime examples: Mile after mile of river that looks pretty much the same. One of our favorite runs on the Deschutes, for example, spans more than half a mile in length.

On this ledge-rock pool on the North Umpqua, the angler is afforded the luxury of utilizing natural "casting platforms" as he works down the river.

Steelhead hold throughout the entire run and yet the surface offers few clues as to the character of the bottom. In other words, this tremendous run is a tough read.

A wider view of the river offers some help however. Below this long run are several hundred yards of fast water where a steelhead will find few holding lies. Thus we are not surprised to find fish throughout the half-mile-long run above. Moreover, as you wade down through this water, you stumble on large rocks and negotiate up, over and around narrow ledges of bedrock running parallel with the current. You soon understand just how much prime holding water is available.

Usually, in fact, the best way to figure out a comparatively featureless river or run is to wade in and fish your way through. For that matter, learn a few basics about reading water then fish your way through with the wet-fly swing: That's the best way to learn any river. As you do so, remember our simplistic description of steelhead water: Between your knees and your eyebrows, maybe a little deeper, and flowing at about the pace you can walk.

A beautiful little "self-mender" pool. Notice how the swift current at the upstream end fans out to create the fishable water to which the angler is casting.

Chapter 6

Wet-Fly Swing Variations: Greased-Lining and Skating

The wet-fly swing can take several variations, these are usually determined by water type and condition. The "greased-line" presentation is one such variation. The wet-fly swing as described previously begins with a "quartering cast" sent down and across stream at an approximate 45-degree angle. The greased-line presentation, conversely, is defined by a cast across and slightly upstream.

Having delivered this cast, you then allow the fly to drift unhindered by drag and you mend line as needed to maintain this drag-free drift. When the fly reaches a point approximating 45-degrees down and across, you fish out the cast by swinging the fly cross-current with or without downstream mends.

The greased-line presentation was originally presented to the Atlantic salmon angling community by A.H.E. Wood in a book titled, *Greased Line Fishing For Salmon.* Writing under the pen name of Jock Scott, Wood presented his greased-line method as a way of fishing salmon under low-water conditions, hence the term low-water fly that accompanies this technique.

The traditional greased-line flies are simple, elegant and beautiful concoctions created by tying a small fly on a proportionately large hook. In other words, one might tie a sparse version of a No. 8 skunk on a size 4 hook. The idea is to present a smallish fly that will not spook skittish steelhead but at the same time offer the fly on a hook capable of fighting and landing fish. Traditionally, the line and leader are greased to float high and dry so the fly will remain just below the surface.

While we won't argue that these sparsely dressed patterns might make the difference once in a while, we feel the greased-line presentation itself is more noteworthy as a fishing tool than are the lovely low-water style flies. In certain pools, we often present our standard patterns on a dead-drift, greased-line cast, the idea being that a steelhead, having viewed the fly in its full broadside width and depth, might be more inclined to give chase than a fish that sees only the narrow profile of a swinging fly. At drifts end we still swing the fly cross-stream.

A perusal of the pools in which we employ this tactic reveals that each shares common characteristics: smooth, flat surface and a comparatively slow, even flow. Such pools, at least in our experience, seem best suited to the greased-line presentation.

Line control constitutes the critical element in this style of fishing because the objective is to accomplish a long, drag-free drift before the fly comes under tension for the cross-current swing. Mending to the downstream side of the fly often allows you to extend this drag-free drift for a considerable distance. Often we set up the cast so that we can use roll mends to lengthen the fly's drift on our downstream side. To do this, first cast across and upstream. As the line lands on the water, keep the rod tip high while reaching up and toward the fly with your casting arm. If needed, throw an upstream mend or two to maintain the drag-free drift. As you do so, maintain the high, extended rod position.

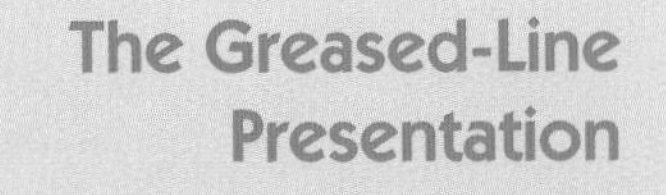

The Greased-Line Presentation

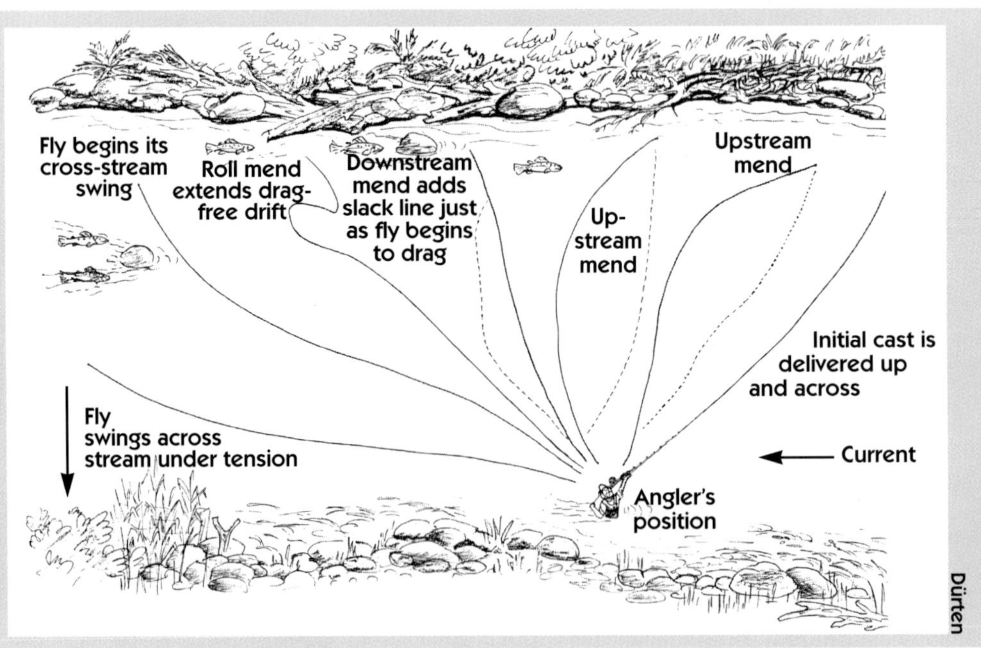

As the fly passes your position, gently remove slack by drawing the rod butt towards you at about forehead level. Now, just before the fly begins to drag, deliver an underpowered roll cast so that a hoop of line rolls about three quarters of the way out toward the fly. Usually this "roll mend" will be delivered to the downstream side of the fly line. Alone, this effective mend will extend the drag-free drift for some distance. To drift the fly even further, reach the rod down toward the fly and slowly release line through the guides. Certainly you can just shake extra line out of the rod guides to help lengthen the drag-free drift during a grease-line presentation, but the roll mend does a better job of setting up the ensuing cross-stream swing.

Naturally, the characteristics of any given flow will determine how best to control and maintain the drag-free drift of your fly on a greased-line cast. Some pools require very little effort to affect this drift while other places demand constant and sometimes complex mending of the line throughout the presentation.

Whatever the case, at least in certain pools, the greased-line presentation is a viable alternative to the standard down-and-across wet-fly swing. No doubt Mr. Wood was correct in determining that this was an effective method for periods of low, clear water when fish might easily be put off by large flies swinging through the currents.

Greased Line or Low-Water Flies

"Low-water" or "reduced" flies are traditionally used for greased-line presentations. Pictured here: low-water Brad's Brat, low-water Del Cooper, low-water Skunk. Virtually any steelhead fly can be tied in this manner.

Included here are a few representative examples of classic-style "low-water" flies traditionally used in conjunction with the greased-line method. We offer these mostly for the sake of interest and curiosity because most of the time we fish our favorite flies even when we employ the greased-line strategy. Still, we feel that these low-water styles make for beautiful dressings. Virtually any classic steelhead fly can be tied in this "reduced" low-water style, so those shown here are a mere sampling of the possibilities.

Low-Water Brad's Brat

Hook: Medium or light wire, No. 2-8
Tag: Gold tinsel
Tail: Orange-dyed golden pheasant crest
Body: 1/2 orange silk, 1/2 red wool or dubbing
Rib: Fine gold tinsel
Throat: Soft brown hackle fibers
Wing: White skunk or polar bear topped with orange

Low-Water Skunk

Hook: Medium or light wire, No. 2-8
Tag: Silver tinsel
Tail: Red-dyed golden pheasant crest
Body: Black silk
Rib: Fine silver tinsel
Hackle: Black
Wing: White

Low-Water Del Cooper

Hook: Medium or light wire, No. 2-8
Tag: Silver tinsel
Tail: Red-dyed golden pheasant crest
Body: Purple silk or wool
Rib: Fine silver tinsel
Throat: Soft red hackle fibers
Wing: White goose shoulder sections

Skating Flies: Steelhead on Top

Whether a subtle boil or a frenzied explosion, the steelhead's rise to a skating dry fly ranks amongst fly fishing's most memorable experiences. Such encounters are made all the more spectacular by their relative scarcity, for only a small percentage of steelhead fly anglers will ever rise a fish to a dry fly.

This is not so much a result of the average steelhead's unwillingness to rise for a dry as it is a natural outcome of so few anglers fishing these flies with regularity. Indeed, steelhead do take dry flies, especially when these flies are fished on a down-and-across swing that allows them to skate slowly across the surface trailing a V-shaped wake. But to take steelhead on the surface, you must be willing to forsake wet flies and instead focus on finding and fishing good dry fly water. You may take a steelhead on top the first day you try; more likely your first dry-fly steelhead will be earned through many hours of diligently skating flies across quiet tailouts and smooth, gliding runs.

We would argue that dry-fly encounters are increasingly rare these days for a very simple reason: Increasing numbers of fly anglers are putting more and more pressure on our summer steelhead rivers, which in turn seems to make the fish themselves increasingly shy and unwilling to chase surface flies. The exception might be British Columbia, where steelhead in several well-known rivers are renowned for their aggressiveness toward dry flies. Yet even on these B.C. rivers, increasing numbers of anglers seem to be finding fewer surface-oriented steelhead.

Bob Hooton, a biologist with the Oregon Department of Fish & Wildlife and a steelhead angler, tells a story of two different seasons on a B.C. river known for its dry-fly fishing: One year he and his party rose steelhead to skating flies seemingly at will, all the while encountering not another angler on the river. A couple years later, with dozens of people on the same stream, they struggled to bring a single fish to the surface. Hence the old steelheading adage makes more sense today than ever: Serious dry-fly anglers had better look for steelhead that have not yet been cast over that day.

None of this is to suggest that all rivers are equal in their potential to produce dry-fly-grabbing steelhead. Some rivers are better than others for dry fly tactics. If, for example, we decided to pursue steelhead on skaters here in Oregon, we would fish the North Umpqua or Deschutes before we would choose any of the other

Deschutes River steelhead.

The skated dry fly presentation begins with a down-and-across cast (A), after which the fly is allowed to swing across the surface, trailing a wake behind (B) (notice the V-shaped wake). Like wet fly fishing, the idea is to control the speed of the fly as it swings cross-current. With the fly being visible throughout the presentation, fishing skaters provides excellent training for wet-fly fishing because the angler can see how different mends and varying currents affect the speed of the fly.

rivers. Theories abound as to why one river offers better surface fishing than another, but no one will ever know for certain.

Nonetheless, steelhead have been hooked on dry flies on all of the Northwest's summer-run rivers at one time or another. Thus if you desire to join the ranks of those who have succeeded in this pursuit, you will find no substitute for honest effort. In other words, put your time in on the river.

Skating tactics are much like wet-fly tactics with the primary goal being to control the speed of the cross-current swing. In fact, fishing the skating fly cannot help but improve your wet-fly technique for the simple reason that, with dry flies, the whole thing is visual. You can watch how different mends and manipulations, currents and flows, affect the speed of the fly as it swings across the pool.

Skating flies are designed to float well enough that the tension from the taut line will not pull them under water. Thus, as they progress cross current on the swing, they trail a subtle wake, hence their other common name "waking flies." Steelhead tend to rise for the fly after this wake has established itself on the surface, but don't automatically assume a hook-up.

Even if you avoid the common mistake of seeing the boil and then immediately setting the hook, which almost always pulls a skating fly away from the rising fish, your chances of a solid hook-up are up for grabs. Despite reacting to the fly, steelhead don't always eat skating flies with sincere conviction. Sometimes they seem more interested in toying with the fly than in actually grabbing it. At times steelhead will lift the fly with their nose, jump over and land on the fly, try to suck it under water, slap it with their flanks or tail, or otherwise do weird, unnerving acts in response to the skater.

Sometimes a steelhead will rise several times in succession for your fly as its travels across stream. Other times a fish will bulge under the fly without breaking the surface. In whatever form it takes, the steelhead's reaction to your skating fly will leave your hands trembling and will also assure you that you have this fish's attention.

Should the fish indeed fail to hook up, make the cast again, perhaps several more times until you are convinced that this steelhead will not rise again. Then switch to a wet fly and fish the area again with the wet-fly swing. Often a fish that shows itself for a skater will take a wet fly on a follow-up cast.

In addition to the standard down-and-across presentation, you can fish surface flies with the greased-line method described previously. With this technique, each cast fishes the fly first as a dead-drift dry fly and then, as drag ensues, as a skating fly. We have watched enough steelhead rise for drifting caddisflies and other insects to know that this dead-drift dry fly approach makes a certain amount of sense, especially as the front half of a skated-fly presentation.

Whatever the case, if you intend to rise a steelhead to a dry fly, you must dedicate yourself to the task. A fishing friend, Matt Abrams, lives in southern California and thus travels to the North Umpqua only once or twice each year. Yet so complete is his affection for rising steelhead to the dry fly that he fishes this way almost exclusively on those infrequent visits to Oregon. That is precisely the dedication required of those who wish to take steelhead on top.

Flies for Surface Fishing

The Bomber, a skating fly originated for Atlantic salmon, has become quite popular amongst steelhead anglers for good reason: It is easy to fish and it brings steelhead to the surface. Moreover, the Bomber is easy to tie, especially if you eliminate the body hackle, which really isn't needed anyway. Along with the Bomber, we carry a handful of other surface patterns, these being listed below.

Bomber

Hook: Lightwire steelhead, No. 2-6
Tail: White calftail or similar

North Santiam River, July.

Body: Spun natural deer hair, trimmed to cigar shape or conical shape
Hackle: Grizzly, palmered through body (optional)
Wing: Same as tail, protruding from the front
Variations: Other colors include orange, black, rust and purple

Giant Stone Skater

Hook: Lightwire steelhead, No. 2-4
Tail: Moose hair or orange Krystal Flash
Body: 1/2 hot orange dubbing, 1/2 fiery brown dubbing
Wing: Natural red squirrel tail hair under natural dark deer or elk. Butt ends from the latter are left to form head
Throat: Orange Krystal Flash

Caddis Flash

Hook: Lightwire steelhead, No. 2-6
Tail: Orange or purple Krystal Flash
Body: Orange or purple Krystal Chenille
Wing: Deer or elk with butt ends left to form head
Throat: Krystal Flash

Grease Liner (Harry Lemire) (not pictured)

Hook: Lightwire, No. 2-8
Tail: Fine natural brown deer hair
Body: Dubbed, usually olive, brown, black or rusty orange
Hackle: Grizzly; sparse
Wing: Same as tail, with butt ends protruding in front of thread wraps to form flared head

Chapter 7

The Transition to Winter Steelhead

Many rivers known for their runs of summer steelhead also host populations of winter steelhead. In fact, some Northwest rivers harbor only winter steelhead. These winter fish constitute a separate race of steelhead. As such, they exhibit a life history different than that of their summer-run brethren.

After returning to the rivers between May and October, summer steelhead wait around until the following winter to spawn during January, February and March. Winter steelhead, meanwhile, typically ascend their native streams between December and March and then go about the business of spawning shortly thereafter. Compared to summer fish, these winter steelhead seem to go about their spawning run with more urgency and less leisure.

Life histories aside, winter steelhead differ in other important ways: Their return to the river coincides with periods of increased flow and decreased water temperatures. Both of these conditions—cold water and heavy flows—affect the behavior of steelhead and in turn influence the way we fish for them.

Generally speaking, winter steelhead react less aggressively to the fly most of the time. The cold water slows the steelhead's metabolism and high, slightly colored water reduces their field of vision. These factors reduce the likelihood that a winter steelhead will chase a fly presented at the surface. Certainly exceptions occur. Sometimes a winter steelhead grabs a fly swinging just below the surface and once in a while a winter fish boils for a skated dry fly. By and large these are indeed the exceptions.

More often, anglers must match their tactics and strategies to the conditions of winter by fishing the fly deeper in the water column where the steelhead is more likely to attack. For all the same reasons we employ it during the summer, the wet-fly swing remains our method of choice for winter fishing. We simply switch to sinking fly lines that allow us to fish the swinging fly deeper than is possible with the floating line.

In fact, winter steelheading brings out the best in the shooting taper system we employ: We can quickly and easily change "heads" to effectively fish different pools and runs. In a deep pool we might choose a fast-sinking, high-density head, but suppose we find the tailout of this pool to be too shallow for such a heavy line? In a matter of minutes we can change to a sink-tip head and fish the remainder of the pool without hanging the fly on the bottom.

We typically carry three different types of sinking heads for winter steelheading. Fast-sinking heads (made from Scientific Anglers Hi-Speed, Hi-D shooting taper lines or from Cortland Type VI or heavier sinking lines) allow us to fish flies near the bottom in the deepest and heaviest flows; we switch to heads made from standard sinking lines (e.g. Cortland Type IV) for pools where the heaviest lines hang up on the bottom. The sink-tip heads, made by chopping the front 30 feet or so from a standard weight-forward, 10-foot sink-tip fly line, allow us to fish the shallower runs and pools without losing flies to the bottom.

The other choice in line systems for winter steelheading is to use full lines with long, heavy sink-tip sections. The lines made by Teeny Nymph Company and by McKenzie Fly Tackle Company, along with similar lines offered by Cortland and Scientific Anglers, all feature long (about 24 feet) high-density sink-tip sections attached by way of a smooth factory splice to a long section of thin-diameter floating line. These are available in several densities, ranging from 120 grains up to 500 grains, thus allowing you to match your line to the prevailing water conditions. The floating "running line" attached to these heavy sink tips allows for easy mending.

No matter which you choose, the primary difference in casting sinking lines and floating lines is that you must strip most of the sinking line in at the end of each presentation in order to lift the fly from the water for the next cast.

We prefer the shooting taper system because of the ease with which we can change lines. To that end, we carry our different heads in a small multi-pouch wallet designed specifically with these coiled heads in mind. This wallet fits easily into a jacket pocket.

Otherwise, both line systems perform similarly with one major exception: The monofilament running line we use to back up our shooting tapers allows for less drag on the surface and thus allows us to slow the fly's swing more effectively and maintain the fly's depth more easily than is possible with the full lines. The floating fly line that backs up the sink-tip lines causes the back end of the sink tip section to suspend away from the bottom, thus increasing the line's drag against the current during the swing. Because of its fine diameter, monofilament running line is quickly pulled down to the level of the sinking line. With less resistance to the current, this monofilament allows for better control of the depth and speed of the fly.

If you opt for a shooting taper system, you must match the weight of your heads to the weight for which your rod is designated. If, for example, you buy a Scientific Anglers 550-grain shooting taper for your nine-weight rod and try to cast the entire 30 feet of this line, all sorts of bad things will happen. Thirty feet of 550-grain fly line is simply too heavy for a nine-weight rod, which is meant to perform ideally with lines that weigh about 240 grains. To cast your 550-grain head effectively you must cut the line down to a length that your rod can handle. If you use Scientific Anglers shooting tapers in the 550-, 700- and 800-grain weights, you will find a chart accompanying the line that shows you how many grains per foot the line weighs. From this chart you

Joe Howell with a North Umpqua steelhead.

Winter steelhead fishing on the North Umpqua.

can simply add the numbers until you arrive at a length that your rod will handle.

Because the specific gravity of any segment of a 550-grain line remains constant, the line will maintain the same sink-rate no matter how long the section. In other words, a 30-foot length of sinking line will sink at the same rate as a five-foot section of the same line (all else being equal). Regardless of its configuration, any shooting taper you create must come close to matching the weight for which your rod is designated to assure efficient, easy casting.

Fly Line Weight Standards

(American Fishing Tackle Manufacturers Association)

Rod Designation	Weight (grains)	Range (Acceptable Tolerance)
7	185	177-193
8	210	202-218
9	240	230-250
10	280	270-290
11	330	318-342
12	380	368-392

The weight designation on a fly rod refers to the weight (in grains) of the line with which that rod will perform best. The table above shows the values assigned to each rod designation from seven-weight through 12-weight. The closer your shooting tapers conform to these values, the better they will perform with your rod.

No matter what kind of sinking line we employ, we typically use leaders in the three- to six-foot length and tippets that test at 10- to 15 pounds. As stated previously, Maxima is our brand of choice. The shorter leaders aid in keeping the fly down during the drift and swing.

As you gain experience in the use of sinking line systems for winter steelhead, you will no doubt find situations that beg deviation from the down-and-across quartering cast. Often, in fact, you can get your fly to the bottom more effectively by casting more cross stream or slightly upstream. Then, as the fly drifts by you can gather slack line in your free hand and then slowly release this line during the swing to control the fly's speed and to maintain its depth.

Naturally your choice of casting angles and the way in which you control the fly's swing, coupled with your choice in line systems, will determine how deep your fly fishes. We are not interested in bumping the fly along the bottom; instead, our experience suggests that a fly fished a foot or two off the bottom results in more strikes. If your fly bangs along on the bottom, hanging on the occasional rock, you might consider lengthening the leader or changing to slower-sinking fly line.

Having made the transition to sinking line systems, you will find winter steelheading to have much in common with summer fishing. The objective is to present the fly on a cross-current swing and to control the speed of the swing. Unlike summer fishing, however, you will swing the fly well below the surface. Having learned and practiced the wet-fly swing during the summer, you need only practice casting the sinking lines to perfect your winter steelhead technique. Reading a river for productive-looking "steelhead water" and then effectively covering these places remains the essential element whether you fish summer or winter.

In fact, winter steelhead offer a reprieve of sorts from the crowded rivers of summer. Comparatively few anglers brave the

Big Deschutes River steelhead. Photo by Rick Wren

elements to pursue winter steelhead on a regular basis, so even our most renowned streams are subject to only a fraction of the pressure commonly associated with the summer runs.

No doubt winter steelheading can seem a lot like work sometimes. If you pick your moments, however, waiting for days when the water drops and when the air is not cruelly cold, you will find winter fishing to be a most pleasant experience.

Best of all, winter steelhead average substantially larger than their summer cousins, with 12- to 15-pound fish being quite common. Moreover these awesome steelhead arrive chrome-bright and full of fight. To bring one to the fly ranks as one of fly fishing's most rewarding encounters.

Flies For Winter Steelhead

Our favorite summer steelhead flies—the Purple Matuka and Spawning Purple—have proven equally effective on winter fish. Thus we stick with these patterns throughout the year. During winter we fish flies as large as size 4/0, but 1/0 and 2/0 would be more typical. Similarly, traditional favorites like the Skunk, Brad's Brat and Skykomish Sunrise make fine choices for the winter season. These too can be fished on large hooks, especially during periods of colored water or very cold water when the steelhead might need a little extra motivation.

Sometimes we fish Spey-style flies during the winter. Such patterns have long been favorites among winter steelhead anglers on the Northwest coast and for good reason: They catch fish. In fact, the Spey-style steelhead flies, originally derived both in form and in name from the classic antique flies fished on Scotland's River Spey, have gained a popular following amongst West-coast tiers. Hence, countless patterns have been introduced into steelhead literature.

Still, many more of these flies adorn the fly plates of books and magazines than drift in front of steelhead. In other words, the number of different Spey-style flies around today far outrepresents the number of such dressings being fished by anglers.

Given the number of and popularity of these Spey-style flies among tiers, the beginning steelheader might well find him or herself at a loss to choose a few good ones. Because of this, we have limited our suggestions to just three representative patterns, these in addition to the aforementioned Orange Heron introduced years ago by the late Syd Glasso (see Chapter 3). The Orange Heron is a rather simple fly for the intermediate tier to master and will prove highly effective on both winter and summer steelhead. As for the countless other steelhead Spey flies, we can only suggest that you choose a fly that seems reasonable and then fish that fly with utter confidence.

In addition, the General Practitioner, an old Atlantic salmon fly designed by Sir Esmund Drury, makes a fine winter steelhead pattern as well. We tie these in the traditional orange, but also in black and purple.

As in our summer steelhead fishing, we prefer to avoid the use of lead-head flies, articulated leeches, nymphs and egg flies. As we've stated before, we consider a steelhead too magnificent a gamefish to be insulted with ugly flies. A beautiful classic steelhead fly hanging from a fish's jaw just prior to release is a sight you won't forget.

So choose a fly that pleases you and then fish with diligence and confidence. Sooner or later you will find a biter and when the fish is on the beach you will marvel at the perfect symmetry of these awesome winter steelhead.

Dressings for Selected Winter Steelhead Flies

Orange Angel (Shewey)

Hook: No. 3/0-2
Body: 1/2 orange silk, 1/2 orange Angora dubbing or similar
Rib: Wide flat gold and fine gold oval
Counter: X-fine gold oval
Hackle: Orange marabou plume with tips dyed black, wound through front half of body following the rib
Collar: Orange-dyed mallard flank
Wing: Two sections of white goose shoulder

Shewey's Black Reeach

Hook: 4/0-2
Butt: Hot orange Angora dubbing or wool
Body: Black; same material as butt
Ribs: Wide gold flat tinsel and small gold oval
Counter: Fine gold oval
Hackle: Blue-eared pheasant rump, dyed black; following rib through body
Collar: Gadwall or teal flank
Wing: Bronze mallard

Midnight Canyon (Shewey)

Hook: 4/0-2
Tag: Gold flat tinsel
Body: 1/2 flat silver tinsel, 1/2 black dubbing
Counter: Fine silver oval or wire
Hackle: Black marabou plume tied Spey-style from the rear, and orange marabou plume with dyed-black tips tied through front half of body only (optional)
Collar: Gadwall flank
Wing: Black goose shoulder segments with two orange strips married through the middle and along the bottom edge of each

General Practitioner (Sir Esmund Drury)

Tag: Flat tinsel
Tail: Polar bear or substitute (dyed white skunk hair) or orange bucktail; tied long
Pincers: Golden pheasant tippet plume with center removed, tied in at mid-shank and topped with two or three golden pheasant flank feathers
Body: Orange dubbing or wool
Hackle: Orange saddle, palmered through body
Rib: Gold oval
Shellback: Three or four more long golden pheasant flank feathers tied in at front and veiling the top of the fly
Note: Substitute black materials or purple materials for black G.P. and purple G.P., respectively; orange pincers add a nice touch to both of these color variations.

Hairwing Spawning Purple (originated by Dave McNeese)

Tag: Gold tinsel
Tail: Orange polar bear or substitute (dyed white skunk or similar), tied long
Body: Orange Angora or seal, loosely dubbed
Wing: Three separate wings of purple-dyed polar bear or substitute, first wing at mid-shank
Collar: Purple hackle followed by natural guinea

LEARN MORE ABOUT FLY FISHING AND FLY TYING WITH THESE BOOKS

If you are unable to find any of these fine books at your local book store or fly shop you can order direct from the publisher below.

TUBE FLIES
A Tying, Fishing & Historical Guide

Mark Mandell & Les Johnson

In the history of fly tying very few books have changed the course of the art. *Tube Flies* will make a very large impact. This all-color, large format book will amaze you with the beauty of tube flies, their ease of tying and very effective fishing traits. Tube flies can be used for everything from stream trout and surface steelhead to billfish. The rich vein of tube fly history, innovation and tying/angling personalities will amaze you and open up an entire new dimension to our sport! 8 1/2 x 11 inches, 96 pages.

SB: $29.95 ISBN: 1-57188-036-4
HB: $45.00 ISBN: 1-57188-037-2

MASTERING THE SPRING CREEKS

John Shewey

Shewey has devoted his life to fly fishing and the quality of his information and photography show it. This sumptuous book featuring full color is an expert's guide to spring creek fly fishing. Everything you need to know from tackle, flies and technique to finding the spring creek you want to fish is included. Many fly plates of the author's recommended best flies and the situations in which to use them. This book is almost as fun as the stream itself—but it will reveal its secrets to you quickly! 8 1/2 x 11 inches, 144 pages.

SB: $24.95 ISBN: 1-57188-000-3
HB: $39.95 ISBN: 1-57188-001-1

AMERICAN NYMPH FLY TYING MANUAL

Randall Kaufmann

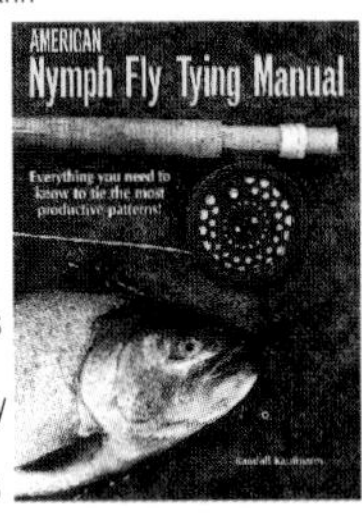

Shows you how to tie 30 of the best nymph patterns. Over 250 photos demonstrate step-by-step. Shown in full color and actual size along with tying instructions are 206 of the most productive nymphs. Color plates show tying materials and colors you need. Hook charts and tying tool photos are included with drawings of various nymphs and explanations of habits. Fishing tips about which to use in different situations. A must book for all trout fly fishermen. 8 1/2 x 11 inches, 93 pages.

SB: $14.95 ISBN: 0-936608-21-8

N.W. FLY FISHING: TROUT AND BEYOND

John Shewey

Shewey rolls back frontiers of Oregon, Washington and Idaho fly fishing for: red-tail surfperch, summer steelhead, chum salmon, striped bass, desert lakes and reservoirs, shad, winter trout streams, saltwater bottomfish, high mountain lakes, char, mackinaw, bull trout, smallmouth bass and sea-run cutthroats. Techniques are explained with many fine drawings, locations and seasons provided, and color fly plates containing many new patterns are shown in large size, with dressings. 8 1/2 x 11 inches, 128 pages.

SB: $21.95 ISBN: 1-878175-24-6
HB: $34.95 ISBN: 1-878175-25-4

ALPINE ANGLER

John Shewey

Sinewy and savvy, John Shewey is one of the west's finest exploring fly fishers. He wrote and photographed this all-color book to help you in your personal discovery of the great trout fishing opportunities that are available for hikers throughout the west from the Rocky Mountains to the Pacific. Everything you need to know: fly fishing methods, hatches, entomology, compass work, map sources. You will want this book for the photography alone! 8 1/2 x 11 inches, 80 pages.

SB: $24.95 ISBN: 1-878175-98-X
HB: $34.95 ISBN: 1-878175-99-8

SALTWATER FLIES: OVER 700 OF THE BEST

Deke Meyer

An all-color fly dictionary of the very best saltwater flies for inshore and ocean use. Effective flies for all saltwater gamefish species. Photographed large, crisp and in true color by Jim Schollmeyer. Pattern recipes next to each fly. This is a magnificent book featuring the largest display of working saltwater fly patterns! 8 1/2 x 11 inches, 119 pages.

SB: $34.95 ISBN: 1-57188-020-8

AMERICAN FLY TYING MANUAL

Dave Hughes

Clear illustrations and photos (83) show you how to tie all 290 patterns in the book which are shown in full color and large size with tying instructions adjacent to each. Best-producing North American flies, including most popular dry, nymph, wet, streamer and bucktail, steelhead, Atlantic salmon, Pacific salmon, cutthroat, Alaskan, saltwater, bass, and panfish patterns. Color plates of tying materials, including fur, hackle, thread, etc. Fly pattern index. Fishing tips for most patterns. Printed on heavy, gloss paper stock. Bound for easy opening. 8 1/2 x 11 inches, 48 pages.

SB: $9.95 ISBN: 0-936608-45-5

STEELHEAD FLY TYING GUIDE

Kent Helvie

This is a gorgeous, all-color, step-by-step book that will make steelhead fly tying easy for you. Scores of crisp color photos show you how to tie all the most productive steelhead patterns including Speys, traditional wets, skaters, wakers and dries. Beautiful color plates will excite you every time you look at them. Once you learn the different tying methods you will then be able to tie all the great patterns shown in the color plates. A magnificent book! 8 1/2 x 11 inches, 80 pages.

SB: $24.95 ISBN: 1-878175-85-8
HB: $34.95 ISBN: 1-878175-86-6

ADVANCED FLY FISHING FOR STEELHEAD

Deke Meyer

All-color book explains the most effective fly fishing techniques for steelhead and the best contemporary flies to use. Chapters on: fly design; Spey flies; wet flies; dry fly; small stream fishing; shooting heads; winter steelheading; two-handed rods; nymphing; deep drifting flies; and much more. Gorgeous book full of fly tying help and material preparation suggestions. Grand color plates of finest producing flies including pattern descriptions. With technique information and fly patterns presented you should be able to successfully fly fish for steelhead anywhere throughout the year. 8 1/2 x 11 inches, 160 pages, all-color.

SB: $24.95 ISBN: 1-878175-10-6

CONCISE HANDBOOK OF FLY TYING

Skip Morris

This is a basic, all-color fly tying guide that teaches all the necessary techniques needed to tie excellent flies for trout and other fish. Tying materials are explained and tying techniques demonstrated. An excellent introductory book to the wonderful world of fly tying! 5 1/2 x 8 1/2 inches, 32 pages.

SB: $7.95 ISBN: 1-57188-035-6

FLIES: THE BEST ONE THOUSAND

Randle Scott Stetzer

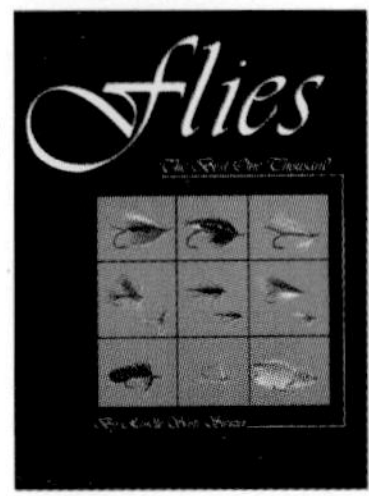

Incredibly beautiful all-color pattern and dressing guide of best flies for trout, salmon, steelhead, bass and saltwater species. Most shown actual size or larger. Marvel at the tiers and photographer's art as you use it over and over researching flies to tie or preparing for a trip. Stetzer is an expert fly tier as well as an expert guide. 8 1/2 x 11 inches, 128 pages.

SB: $24.95 ISBN: 1-878175-20-3

TYING FOAM FLIES

Skip Morris

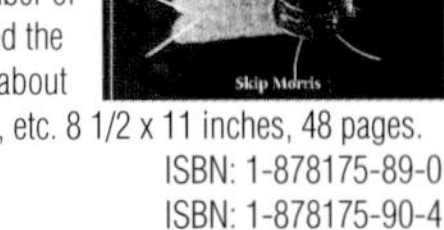

This is the first book done about how to tie fascinating, productive foam flies and all photos are in color. Master fly tier Skip Morris shows you step-by-step in clear photos and descriptive text how to make buggy- looking foam flies that are at the forefront of fly fishing development. With this easy to understand book you will be able to create any number of new patterns after you have learned the tying step. Thorough information about types of foam, best threads, knots, etc. 8 1/2 x 11 inches, 48 pages.

SB: $16.95 ISBN: 1-878175-89-0
HB: $29.95 ISBN: 1-878175-90-4

FLY TYING MADE CLEAR AND SIMPLE

Skip Morris

Expert tier Skip Morris shows how easy it is to tie excellent flies in this all-color book. Over 220 color photographs show all the techniques you need to know. 73 different materials in color plus 27 tools. Clear, precise advice tells you how to do it step-by-step as well as pointing out difficulties and explaining how to overcome them! Dries, wets, streamers, nymphs, etc., included so that you can tie virtually any pattern. 8 1/2 x 11 inches, 80 pages.

SB: $19.95 ISBN: 1-878175-13-0
HB: $29.95 ISBN: 1-878175-14-9

THE ART OF TYING THE NYMPH

Skip Morris

This is the finest book available for tying nymphs. Totally illustrated in color with over 400 step-by-step photographs. Learn to tie all nymphs from simple to very complex. Skip Morris carefully guides you step-by-step. Ninety nymphs shown in color with dressings allow you to match virtually all naturals for any fishing situation. Large format stays open easily. Morris is also one of the world's finest display fly tiers, guaranteeing you learn from a master. 8 1/2 x 11 inches, 112 pages.

SB: $29.95 ISBN: 1-878175-51-3

THE ART OF TYING THE DRY FLY

Skip Morris

This is the finest book ever published concerning how to tie dry flies featuring over 400 clear, color photos demonstrating all the techniques and materials you need, plus the clear, concise tying instructions from display-fly tier Skip Morris. Contains the information you need to tie the very best 100 dry flies—a dry fly for virtually ANY stream occasion you will meet! Printed on bright, glossy paper, large format which stays open easily. 8 1/2 x 11 inches, 112 pages.

SB: $29.95 ISBN: 1-878175-36-X
HB: $39.95 ISBN: 1-878175-37-8

VISA, MASTERCARD ORDERS CALL TOLL FREE; 1-800-541-9498 (9-5 PACIFIC STANDARD TIME)

OR SEND CHECK OR MONEY ORDER TO:

FRANK AMATO PUBLICATIONS, INC. • PO BOX 82112 • PORTLAND, OREGON 97282

(PLEASE ADD $3.00 FOR SHIPPING AND HANDLING)